WHEN FISH FLY

WHEN FISH FLY

Lessons for Creating a Vital and Energized Workplace
from the World Famous Pike Place Fish Market

JOHN YOKOYAMA,
Owner of the World Famous Pike Place Fish Market

JOSEPH A. MICHELLI, PH.D.

HYPERION NEW YORK

Library of Congress Cataloging-in-Publication Data

Yokoyama, John.
    When fish fly : lessons for creating a vital and energized workplace from the world famous Pike Place Fish Market / John Yokoyama, Joseph Michelli.
        p. cm.
    ISBN 1-4013-0061-8
    1. Employee motivation. 2. Customer services. 3. Success in business. 4. World Famous Pike Place Fish (Seattle, Wash.) I. Michelli, Joseph A. II. Title.
    HF5549.5.M63Y65 2004
    658.3'14—dc22   2003056771

Hyperion books are available for special promotions and premiums. For details contact Michael Rentas, Manager, Inventory and Premium Sales, Hyperion, 77 West 66th Street, 11th floor, New York, New York 10023-6298, or call 212-456-0133.

FIRST EDITION

10 9 8 7 6 5 4 3 2

| A C K N O W L E D G M E N T S |

Johnny and I are deeply indebted to our families (Diane and Stacy Yokoyama, and Nora, Andrew, and Fiona Michelli) for the sacrifices they have made throughout our careers and during the writing of this book.

While Johnny has opportunities to talk about his family throughout the book, this is my only chance. I wish to acknowledge Nora's steadfast commitment to and support of me, our family, and this project. She has held the family together through my many absences. Andrew and Fiona have lost much "Daddy Time" to Seattle and Pike Place Fish. May we make it up one hundredfold.

When Fish Fly would not have taken shape without the wisdom and guidance of Jim Bergquist and the support of Karen Bergquist and the entire bizFutures staff.

We are grateful for the commitment of the crew of Pike Place Fish and the assistance they offered with this project.

Special thanks to Will Schwalbe for his faith in this book, Mark Chait for his consistent encouragement and exceptional editorial skill, the entire team at Hyperion, and our counsel, David Lenci and Lloyd Rich.

I want to also thank all those who reviewed the manuscript and/or listened to me drone on about the ideas and stories contained herein.

A heartfelt thank you to my assistant, Mimi Cromer, for all the reviews and innumerable tasks involved in helping this book take flight.

—Joseph A. Michelli, Ph.D.

|CONTENTS|

|1|

Creating a Vision of Power and Possibility: 1
Seeing the Big Fish

|11|

Achieving Individual Commitment and Team Alignment: 17
Rowing as One

|111|

Focusing on the Process for Achieving Success: 37
It's Not about the Fish, It's about the Experience of Fishing

|1V|

Changing Yourself First: 57
Breaking Free from the Net

| V |

Choosing Powerful Conversations: 71
Removing the Hook

| VI |

Making a Difference by Listening Intently: 85
Hush, or the Fish Won't Bite

| VII |

Coaching for Greatness: 105
From Minnows to Whales

| VIII |

Turning Workplace Challenges into Breakthroughs: 123
Unsnagging the Line

| IX |

Taking a Stand: 139
Finding Your Fish Worth Catching

Credits   157

WHEN FISH FLY

Creating a Vision of Power and Possibility

Seeing the Big Fish

FROM BANKRUPTCY TO WORLD FAME

FOR TWENTY YEARS, I WORKED HARD to make my business—a small fish stand in Seattle's Pike Place Market—successful. During much of that time, I didn't take vacations and was on the job twelve hours a day, six days a week. Like many small businesses, my company wasn't a huge success. My hard work and that of my employees resulted in a decent lifestyle for all of us, but I wanted something more for the Pike Place Fish Market. I considered expanding my business.

Around 1986, I decided to venture into the wholesale side of the fish industry. It was a huge mistake! I delegated responsibility for our wholesale operation to a person who put me seriously in debt in just nine months. My business and I were in trouble.

Unless I could get $50,000 quickly, the Pike Place Fish Market would face bankruptcy. Because I hadn't borrowed money from banks in the past, I couldn't get a loan when I needed it. Fortunately, my mother-in-law came through with the money. I pulled my team together and told them, "It's either sink or swim." We decided to swim, and we stabilized financially.

Around the same time a friend, Karen Bergquist, called and suggested that I talk with her husband, Jim, a business consultant, about Pike Place Fish's future. When I met with Jim, he told me he had a unique approach to consulting. Unfortunately, his fee was more than I paid a full-time employee who worked sixty hours a week. I told him, "You must be crazy!" There was no way I was going to pay someone that much to "consult" with us. Jim told me that if I tried his services for three months and he didn't produce what I invested in him, I should fire him. So I took a chance that he could help me create a more profitable future. He and his company have now been working with us for seventeen years.

Jim brought our staff together in crew meetings every other week to empower us. It was at one of these meetings that he helped us appreciate that we were thinking too small and that we needed a bigger purpose—a bigger game. One crewmember's response to that challenge was, "Let's become world famous!" World famous? Us? What does *that* mean? It seemed like a ridiculous idea. We were a 1,200-square-foot fish stand, just recovering from financial disaster. The only way I was going to go for being world famous was if it didn't cost me any money. We had no money to market ourselves; how could we be "world famous"? But rather than giving up on the idea, we decided to explore it further.

We didn't want to just take some standard notion of world

fame. We needed to create the concept for *us*, in *our* workplace. When we first began to brainstorm, some amusing ideas surfaced. One fishmonger imagined that if we were world famous, we would all be coming down to the market in business suits, driving our Mercedeses. We would purchase a pier and operate the fish market from an office building.

But as we continued to contemplate the meaning of world fame as it related to us, it became clear that we intended to make a world famous difference by having a positive impact upon each person we encountered. To this day, we continue to define world fame as situations come up at the market. What is it to be world famous, for example, when things are slow at work? What does world famous look like when customers treat us badly?

As we discussed world fame, we realized that by working together, we could affect each other's lives and the lives of our customers in a world famous way. We could achieve limitless results. Individually, we committed to create "World Famous Pike Place Fish." It was a vision that gave us a powerful purpose for doing business. What initially seemed like an outrageous idea caught fire with the team. As Jim puts it, "We created World Famous Pike Place Fish, and what it meant to be world famous was to make a difference for the people we touched. The purpose wasn't just to be famous. It was to be famous for being great with people—for free—just for the fun of it. And that's what happened."

With the declaration of World Famous Pike Place Fish, we evolved from a company that existed totally to sell fish to one that was interested in extraordinary service to our customers and our world. Selling fish was no longer the main reason we were

"If you want to build a ship, don't drum up the men to gather up the wood, divide the work and give orders. Instead, teach them to yearn for the vast and endless sea."

—ANTOINE DE
SAINT-EXUPÉRY

open for business. Don't get me wrong—when you visit the market, we will provide you the highest-quality fish and in turn take your money and put it in our cash register. Like all small businesses, an important part of our game is to make a profit. But making a profit is not enough. If a manager or owner is interested only in making a profit, then the lens through which he looks at his employees allows him to see only their ability to help him achieve financial success. When the game goes beyond profit to a greater purpose, workers are valued for their ability to create profit *and* serve others. As a result of our vision, the fish are now only a means to an end. Selling fish gives us an opportunity to make a world famous difference—and for that I am grateful.

Our vision is large enough and clear enough that it guides our staff in day-to-day operations. It generates a more meaningful reality for all of our employees. They are not simply fish salespeople; they are agents of change. Anyone can sell fish—few can make a world famous difference while doing it.

I can attest to the power of a purposeful vision—breakthroughs happen. Looking past the everyday demands of the bottom line, we continually seek to live our vision, World Famous Pike Place Fish. For us, the vision *is* the bottom line. If World Famous Pike Place Fish is present through us, all else falls into place.

MY THREE PLEDGES AS OWNER

It is very clear to me what World Famous Pike Place Fish means. From my perspective as the owner, I will:

1. Make a world famous difference in the lives of everyone who comes into my business;

2. Empower the creative people I work with so that they can make a world famous difference for each other, the customers, the community, and beyond; and

3. Demonstrate what is possible when you empower your employees. (Originally, my desire was to demonstrate this only to small-business owners. These days, I also find myself sharing these possibilities with executives in large corporations, as well as with organizations and community leaders.)

Sometimes my intentions are difficult to live. Although I have committed to them, I must admit that I am not always *being* World Famous Pike Place Fish. Some days I struggle just to get to work. But even when I am not being purposeful, I know I am capable of finding my way back to my commitments. I choose where I am at a given moment, and I always have the choice to bring myself back to the vision.

With every customer, every crewmember, every supplier, and even with you, the reader, I have the choice to live World Famous Pike Place Fish. When I miss opportunities to enhance the lives of my customers or crew, I am very aware of the choices I've made. I can't excuse myself from responsibility by saying, "I don't know what our purpose means." I can't avoid accountability by saying, "I am the boss, so this world famous thing doesn't apply to me." My staff knows that I share the vision; not only have I said so formally and publicly, but I regularly recommit to it. In my own head, on a moment-to-moment basis, I reconfirm that I am "John Yokoyama, World Famous Pike Place Fish."

HOW TO TURN AROUND A HOSTILE WORKPLACE

Once upon a time, the Pike Place Fish Market was a pretty hostile work environment. I remember yelling so much that I made one fishmonger start to cry. Through his tears, he said, "I can never make you happy!" When I wasn't happy, the whole Pike Place Market area knew it. Given the way I treated people in those days, Pike Place Fish was a revolving door for employees; they left about as quickly as they arrived. We had significant problems with employee theft, staff drunkenness, and drug use. If we weren't fighting with one another, we were getting into physical fights with vagrants who tried to steal fish from the stand. In the middle of all this chaos, we were the next to last in profitability of all the fish shops in the Pike Place Market. Since we began changing our culture, not only are we consistently at the top of fish sales in the market, it would be difficult to find any retail store in America that makes more money per square foot of retail space. The stability of our staff has been outstanding, as we haven't had a full-time employee leave within the past five years. In fact, believe it or not, we have people volunteer to work one day a week with us just to experience our culture.

We have a saying at the fish market, "The fish stinks from the head." Unfortunately, I have always been the head of this fish company, so when things smell around here, it starts with me. While it might be easy to blame the problems the fish market used to experience on my staff or other business factors, my attitude shaped our culture. It wasn't until I chose a different way of relating to my employees through our vision that things truly began to change. Once I understood the creative power of people and the importance of offering a place where they could make a difference, Pike Place Fish began to take off. I used to run the fish market as a dictator and seldom a benevolent one. Even now, we don't run as a democracy. Our crewmembers share ideas and create suggestions, but because I have the greatest financial stake in the outcome, the final decisions rest with me.

In the early days of World Famous Pike Place Fish, I had modest intentions. I wanted my business to succeed and maybe show other business owners what happens when you love and empower your employees. Later on, I understood that my store could make a real difference in people's lives and in the world. We've come to learn that achieving fame and being "World Famous Pike Place Fish" are two very different things. Our intention was not to bring fame to ourselves. Instead, it was to deliver as world famous fishmongers would. As is always the case, the intentions from which you work bring forth powerful and unpredictable results.

CREATING SUCCESS FOR OTHERS GENERATES FAME FOR YOU

Through our vision and our willingness to incorporate that vision into our moment-to-moment encounters, Pike Place Fish has enjoyed more than its share of attention, and what draws many people to us is that our fishmongers throw fish to one another. Shortly after we defined our vision, the Goodwill Games came to Seattle. Photographers and news crews from places as diverse as China, Japan, Zaire, Russia, and Germany trained their cameras on our energized workers. As our fishmongers threw fish and delighted the crowds, the world looked on. Without our spending a dime, stories and pictures of our Pike Place fishmongers were appearing everywhere.

Shortly after the Goodwill Games, a movie producer came to us and told us that he had seen our fishmongers on television during the games. He proceeded to hire three members of our staff to throw fish in the movie *Free Willy*. After that, ABC's *Good Morning America* contacted us to be on their show through a live feed. The staff's world famous efforts were obvious as they came down at four o'clock in the morning to set up the fish market so it could be seen in its full glory.

One of our team members was living "World Famous Pike Place Fish" while watching television from his home. During an MTV program, he heard that Spike Lee was filming a new Levi's commercial, and he wanted to use people with interesting jobs. The fishmonger joined 650,000 other entries, and Spike Lee chose us as a location for one of his jeans commercials.

We changed our shipping box and signs around the market by adding the words "World Famous." And the strangest thing began to happen. Not only were we publicly stating our vision, but strangers were communicating it as well. I would stand in the crowd and listen to people as they watched the crew in action. They would talk to one another and say things like, "Wow, these guys are world famous!" Or, "I heard about these guys. They are the World Famous Pike Place Fish guys." We declared that we were world famous, and other people actually took the idea and spread it.

When Nordstrom relocated their downtown Seattle store in 1998, they depicted the community through pictures of the faces of citizens and highly visible Seattle fixtures. These pictures were wrapped around their newly renovated building location. One of the images presented on their building wraps was the face of a World Famous Pike Place Fishmonger.

At one of our meetings, my brother, Dicky, our closet actor, said, "It's time for us to have *Pike Place Fish: The Movie* show up." Most of us looked at him and laughed, saying, "Yeah, right!" After further discussion, we collectively encouraged one another to share our message as broadly as possible.

Within a month, John Christensen of ChartHouse Learning stopped by the market. He was in town doing a video about a poet, David Whyte, who lived on nearby Whidbey Island. As John walked by the fish market, he saw the energy and vitality. One of our mongers took the time to "make a difference" with John. He found out that John made educational videos, and together they discussed the possibility of John making a video about World Famous Pike Place Fish. Shortly thereafter, John contacted me with an interest in making a corporate training video about us. We didn't think too much of it because people take videos at the market all the time. I told John that he was welcome to make a video. John brought his entire crew from Minnesota and filmed us every day for a week. We still hadn't appreciated the importance of this project. Then John signed a contract with us, returned to Minnesota, and called us back three months later. John told me, "I have completed the video and would like to show it to you and the guys." John came to Seattle, took us to dinner, and we previewed the produced video.

We were impressed with the video but thought it was a little short, only seventeen minutes. Then we really began to worry about John when he told us he was going to be selling it for $599. We said, "Man, that's too much! You aren't going to sell any of them. Who is going to pay that kind of money?" We were coming from the perspective of what videos cost in a video store, $20 to $25 each. We had no idea about corporate video sales and rentals, or about ChartHouse Learning's distribution and John's worldwide market.

Within a year, that video, *Fish!*, became the hottest selling corporate training video and was translated into thirteen foreign languages. John Christensen came back the next year and requested the opportunity to make another video, and *Fish! Sticks* was taped.

Sprint, Marriott, Ford Motor Company, Panasonic, and thousands of other companies purchased these training videos from ChartHouse Learning. *Fish!* looks at several components involved in the energy of our culture, while *Fish! Sticks* examines how we maintain alignment with our vision.

Everything started to pop when those videos were released. People from different corporations came up every day and talked to us about the videos. Often people arrived in groups. Companies would send their employees to check us out to see if we were for real. Lots of times these people would just stand in the crowd and watch us before they came up and introduced themselves.

Despite all the attention, we continued to stay our course and live our vision by maximizing our focus on the person who was in front of us at the time and doing all we could for him or her. About this time, *Fast Company* magazine interviewed us for an article about our people and business philosophy. Immediately after that, three local television programs interviewed us. Requests for newspaper interviews flooded in from across the country. Even *People* magazine showed up and did two pages filled with pictures about the fishmongers. How do a bunch of fishmongers get a spread in *People* magazine? We hadn't called anybody. We were World Famous Pike Place Fish, and we hadn't spent a dime on advertising.

What's next after *People* magazine? I've come to learn that when you create a vision, the universe will let you know what's to come. We started getting e-mails from companies asking if we did speeches. I told each person who expressed an interest that we didn't offer speaking services. When people asked me to speak, I was quick to tell them, "I am not a speaker. I am a fish-market owner." At our regular meetings, I let the staff know how many inquiries (three or four a week) we were getting concerning speeches. Finally, the requests came in so regularly that crewmembers said, "Hey boss, we have to do this speaking stuff." I reluctantly agreed, on the condition that I would never travel to do a speech. I hate traveling.

Jim Bergquist, a couple of fishmongers, and I did our first presentation for a Seattle real estate management company. When they asked how much we charged for an hour-long presentation, I had no idea what to ask as a fair price. As time went on, our local presentations increased. Jim took over the speaking business and we created a separate training company called Flying Fish/bizFutures. Unfortunately for me, inquiries for out-of-town presentations became overwhelming. I kept refusing to travel, but Jim advised me that we needed to take the presentations on the road. Finally, at a crew meeting, the team decided to "create a world famous difference by speaking around the country and the world." So I packed my bags. Our speaking fees continue to climb, and our message continues to be warmly and eagerly received. Now we have expanded our services to include two-day courses here in Seattle. They are produced by consultants from bizFutures and utilize the fishmongers and the fish market as part of the training.

I find it strange that when we first explored the possibility of "World Famous Pike Place Fish" we had no idea what this vision would actually look like. We just knew we wanted to make a difference, increase our profits, and stand out internationally for our efforts. I marvel at the magnificent manner in which world fame has presented itself to us. The opportunities continue to unfold. Since the first two videos, John Christensen has produced a third video entitled *Fish! Tales,* which examines the impact that aspects of our business approach have had on companies and industries as wide-ranging as telecommunications, automobile sales, and health care.

In March 2000, a fictionalized story was published. It was inspired by Pike Place Fish and explored how a manager turned around an uninspired workplace. The book, *Fish! A Remarkable Way to Boost Morale and Improve Results,* was written by Steve Lundin, Ph.D., John Christensen of ChartHouse Learning, and Harry Paul. There are over 1.5 million copies in print (at the time of this publication) and the book has made every major business bestseller list, including the *Wall Street Journal, USA Today*, the *New York Times, Business Week, Publishers Weekly,* and Amazon.com. *Fish!* has also reached the bestseller lists in Japan, Germany, Spain, and Korea and has regularly appeared on Amazon.com's Top 100 Seller list (reaching number one). It is licensed for publication in thirty-four languages. In 2002, the sequel book, *Fish! Tales*, was launched, and in 2003, *Fish! Sticks* was published. Both of these books were met with great reviews and robust sales.

The fame of our Pike Place fishmongers continues to draw the attention of the world. Two of my guys attained a "world record" and appeared on *The Guinness Book of World Records* television program for throwing the most fish a distance of eighteen feet in thirty seconds—twenty-six fish in total. Later, they were flown to Munich, Germany, to compete in and win a German world-record fish-throwing event. Pike Place Fish has been on ESPN sports programming, *CBS Sunday Morning* with Charles Osgood, and the *Frasier* program on NBC. One of the people on MTV's *Real World Seattle*, David, became a fishmonger as he shared the twists and turns of his life on reality television and further exposed Pike Place Fish to a young television audience. Similarly, a couple of our fishmongers were on the television show *Elimidate*. The great business cartoonist Scott Adams had fun with the idea that a fish market would have something to say about a productive business culture.

Wheel of Fortune has used the World Famous Pike Place Fish crew in its show in a variety of ways, including throwing fish to

DILBERT reprinted by permission of United Feature Syndicate, Inc.

Vanna White. She is just one of many celebrities who have either thrown or caught our fish. Even I have appeared on the game show *To Tell the Truth*. I am, however, still waiting for a good movie deal about the market and to see who will play me in the World Famous Pike Place Fish feature-length movie. And to think that all of this came to us by living our vision and maintaining our focus on making a difference, one person at a time.

Achieving Individual Commitment and Team Alignment

Rowing as One

COMMITTING TO THE VISION

I AM 100 PERCENT COMMITTED TO our vision. Of course, I should be—I am the owner. What is unusual about Pike Place Fish is that we have created a place where the entire crew is invested in making a world famous difference. As new staff joins us, we create opportunities for them to share our vision. It all starts with an invitation period that typically lasts three months. Normally after that period, we decide whether the person is a fit for us, and he decides whether to make a public commitment—in the form of a declaration to all crewmembers—to our vision.

I've noticed that many business owners spend a lot of time teaching people how to perform their jobs and far less time explaining the greater purpose of the work. Sometimes employees become aware of their company's mission simply by being told to "read the policy manual." I guess these employers think that workers will just "get" the mission without being coached on how to bring the company's purpose alive on the job. I've begun to wonder, after so many well-published scandals, whether the people who run many of these large companies understand and live their own mission and values.

Employees don't experience ownership of a vision when they are *required* to subscribe to it. Most employees will act as though they live the vision, at least when a manager is watching. Compliance, however, is not the same as buying into the values and mission of the organization.

Our approach at Pike Place Fish is to spend considerable time discussing and sharing our vision of making a world famous difference. Employees aren't asked to read about our vision. We don't even have a vision statement written down or hung on a wall. Our vision is our daily work life! If you aren't willing to consistently make a world famous difference, then our job is not for you. I'd never want someone to be placed in a situation where they work at Pike Place Fish *only* to get a paycheck.

When people explore the possibility of working with us, I serve as a resource to them. Specifically, I help prospective employees author their own vision of World Famous Pike Place Fish. They are challenged to align their personal vision of making a world famous difference with the vision shared by the rest of the team. When I talk to prospective employees about World Famous Pike Place Fish, I offer them a particular opportunity to alter the way they see the world. It is their choice whether or not to accept my very personal invitation.

I want new hires to bring their creative nature to Pike Place Fish. I call on them to share their unique gifts and talents and not simply to bring a set of technical skills. They are encouraged to create opportunities at Pike Place Fish that reflect their purpose in living—namely, to positively affect the world—an effect that radiates throughout Seattle and beyond, all from our little fish stand. If it sounds strange to you, think about how odd it might be for a twenty-year-old single male—the most common Pike Place Fish job candidate. My invitation is certainly not right for everyone, and I am glad when people honestly and thoughtfully turn it down.

At Pike Place Fish, commitment to our common goal is a critical element in our success. We make the offer of employment to those who understand and share our passion for service. It is not a one-time-only offer—sign up now, or it is gone. The offer results from an orientation journey. The invitation emphasizes our "intention" and "commitment" to help job candidates decide whether they want to join the team, and whether the team and its vision are a fit for them.

HELPING STAFF FIND THE OPPORTUNITY TO SERVE

Jim Bergquist and I meet with our entire staff every other week. We bring the staff together at a dinner to discuss our vision, invite enrollment, and stay aligned with the vision. While twice-monthly meetings of the entire crew might seem like a large time commitment and expense, we view our dinners as essential for staying "on purpose."

While many employers spend a lot of time looking for the "best, brightest, and most talented" job applicants, we are looking for people who are willing and able to change. In essence, we believe that people's greatest work asset is their willingness to look at themselves, accept feedback, and grow personally.

After filling out an application, job candidates meet with one of our managers. Those prospective employees who get a chance at a job tend to be the most persistent applicants. They keep coming back weekly to see whether there is an opening. Our new hires *don't* have to have a background working with fish or in sales. We aren't looking for fish salesmen—we want team members who can take responsibility for their own actions and consistently *be* World Famous Pike Place Fish.

At first we don't talk much about our vision. New people are simply thrown into the culture. My initial expectation is rather basic. I want a new hire to show up for work on the first day—usually a Saturday. Saturday is the busiest and most overwhelming day at the market. The pace is hectic, with swarms of customers encircling. Most people make it to work, but not all of them survive the first day. We've literally had people come in on a Saturday morning, leave for their lunch break, and never come back. It's just that crazy.

From the beginning, we let prospective employees know that they will have to make the team and that team membership will require a great capacity for growth. At first, we have our new hires do things like shovel ice and perform "gofer" work. When they step into our rubber boots for their first day, they instantly appreciate the overwhelming physical and mental nature of the work. They quickly realize that there are many easier ways to make money!

Who do you know who wants to work fifty-two hours a week? Our crew is on the job at 6:30 A.M. preparing the show (the fish displays). They set up displays with 2,500 to 3,000 pounds of fish, move and shovel carts of ice, strain their backs, and freeze their hands and feet. Sometimes it is so cold and damp that the skin on the fishmongers' hands literally cracks open. The fish display is ready by eight in the morning, although the fishmongers are ready to serve customers even while preparing the show. The day is a buzz of activity, interacting with passersby, engaging customers, throwing and catching fish, shouting back and forth to one another, restocking the display, wrapping, packaging, shipping, and then tearing down at six in the evening—in the hope of leaving by 6:30 P.M. Of course, team members do get a thirty-minute lunch break and two fifteen-minute rest periods. Otherwise, they are on their feet for eleven hours. I can assure you, I can't pay people enough to want to do the job. I am not sure whether I would want to work with the type of person who would be willing to endure the job only for the pay.

CELEBRATE PEOPLE, AND YOUR RECRUITING WORRIES ARE GONE

Despite the physical demands and pace of working at the fish market, we always have a waiting list of people who want to sign on with us. We've never had to advertise for fishmongers. Most people seek employment either because they've seen us in action or because they have heard we are a unique and positive place to work. Frequently, a current employee encourages a friend to submit an application. Other times, people come right out of the

"Never doubt that a small group of thoughtful, committed citizens can change the world; indeed, that is the only thing that ever has."

— MARGARET MEAD

crowd and ask for a job. Many people apply because of a powerfully positive experience they had with a member of our staff. In essence, the applicant experienced a world famous difference, and they want to join the team.

Most people arrive with a sense that we are doing something unusual. Some people think we are a uniquely "fun" group of guys, others like the idea that we entertain people by throwing fish. We don't formally share our vision until a new hire attends his first staff meeting. We make it clear that we don't have jobs, just openings for people who share our vision. We emphasize the importance of attending the meetings (they are mandatory) and ask the new hires to willingly listen and be open to discovering that they make a difference in their own lives and in the lives of those around them. We emphasize that they will have the choice to commit or not commit to our vision in about three months, and that we will give them time to understand what it truly means to be World Famous Pike Place Fish.

When we present at business conferences, business owners frequently ask me, "How can we get our people to behave in accord with our vision?" These well-intentioned owners don't realize that they are actually asking, "How do I persuade people to do what they may not want to do, and instead do what I want them to do?"

At Pike Place Fish, we view people in a very different way. People are *not* objects to be motivated or persuaded into action. Fundamentally, people are creative beings! Once you accept that powerful creativity of employees, you simply need to present the opportunity for them to grow and generate. For me, that is as simple as creating a new, exciting reality with them. I invite new hires to step into that new reality with the rest of the team and me. In a general sense, the new reality being offered at Pike Place Fish goes something like this:

> You can come to work and affect the world for the better. You can matter in the lives of others. You can share a powerful vision with our team and create break-through success, and, yes, you can do all that while throwing and selling fish.

As I offer this new possibility, I acknowledge that the new hire will have to creatively provide the details of how he will personally bring the vision to life at Pike Place Fish. I encourage people to choose or decline the shared vision. My invitation implies a promise. If they accept the invitation, I am extending a commitment to support them. That means I assist them, even if their way of living the vision is very different from my own. To maintain my integrity, I have to live into the commitment extended through the offer, just as they have to live into their commitment for the vision.

OPENING UP TO EMPLOYEE IDEAS

Sometimes when people accept the offer and start generating ideas and suggestions about how to improve the business, I find myself reluctant to honor my commitment. An employee will bring up a suggestion, and I will immediately think, "No way. We aren't doing that." But after I have time to see that the suggestion is coming from the uniqueness of my employee's perspective and out of a willingness and desire to live our vision of World Famous Pike Place Fish, I usually see the good in the idea and how it might work. So when the fishmongers approached me and suggested that we create a line of Pike Place Fish merchandise, I asked them to explore it. They came back with a proposal for a pilot project involving their design of a Pike Place Fish baseball cap to be sold at the market and on our website. In discussing the possibility, they asked to create both the design and the production of the cap and have me provide the initial capital. We discussed profit sharing from the proceeds of the cap and other possible products like key chains, cups, and a cookbook written by the fishmongers. Given their efforts in exploring and creating the caps, I provided the needed money. Thanks to the fishmongers, we have a wide range of merchandise available at the market these days.

At another point, the team proposed a webcam so that visitors to our website could experience the real-time antics of the market from the comfort of their own homes. While I initially had difficulty understanding the benefit of this and justifying the cost, we've consistently gotten great feedback from web users about the camera. We even have people reporting that they watch our live webcam at www.pikeplacefish.com on a daily basis.

Another idea that initially met with my resistance was the suggestion an employee made that our typical sixty-hour work-week be reduced to fifty-two hours. At first, I thought, "This is not a suggestion consistent with World Famous Pike Place Fish. He wants me to reduce the crew's workweek by eight hours and not reduce salaries. It just can't work." Fortunately, I looked at my commitment to honor and support my employees' efforts to create greatness and suggested that I could support the idea of a fifty-two-hour workweek if the entire team created a plan that met two conditions: (1) they would be responsible for working out scheduling and coverage issues; and (2) there would be no drop in sales or profitability. As is typically the case when you encourage creativity and teamwork, the crew produced a highly effective schedule that not only met my criteria but improved profitability in the process.

As our employees have generated their personal visions of making a world famous difference, and I have supported those visions, the market has truly transformed. Just think, my company has been picked by CNN as America's Most Fun Place to Work. Before our shared commitment to the vision, Pike Place Fish might have been in the running for being one of the *least* fun places to work.

As the owner, I let new hires know that I have taken responsibility for the longevity and success of this business, and I will make sure Pike Place Fish continues to exist in the world. This means that even in the three slowest months of the year, when I lose money, I don't lay people off. It means that health, dental, and vision coverage is not only paid for each team member but that our employees have no out-of-pocket expenses for these services. I have had to reinvent myself from a person who saw employees simply as a means to an end into one who profoundly cares about their well-being. My promise to my employees is at the foundation of our success. My commitment to our people is essential in a time when corporations often expect loyalty from their employees with little assurance of support and security offered in return. I also affirm that I am devoted to having my business and the people in it make a profound difference. In essence, my invitation to my employees can be summarized as follows:

> We are on a journey, and we have been on this journey for more than fifteen years. We are committed to this, and everybody who works here has personally taken responsibility for participation and for being on this boat. Committing to working here means you are not just accepting a job. If you take a stand to be on this team, you are declaring that you will make a difference for every customer and have a positive, world famous impact on the world at large. If you say "yes" to working here, you become an owner and creator of this vision. What that means personally for you is that you *are* World Famous Pike Place Fish. You are generating the whole thing from your place in the universe.

CLARIFYING WHAT COMMITMENT MEANS

Prior to accepting my invitation, new employees examine what it means to make a commitment. Just as many couples participate in premarital counseling to examine the commitment of marriage, we talk about what the commitment to World Famous Pike Place Fish means. Once a fishmonger understands the vision, he needs to look at how he can overcome barriers that might limit his ability to *be* the vision.

For example, we had an eighteen-year-old fishmonger who was very shy and would typically avoid eye contact. When discussing how he wanted to grow in his ability to make a difference, he noted that he wanted to be able to sell like one of our lead salespeople. Instead of reacting with "Fat chance! You can't even look the customers in the eye," we talked about his willingness to re-create himself to be powerfully present with customers. He expressed a strong commitment to that opportunity for growth. Likewise, the team committed to support him in that journey. In fact, one of our superstar sales guys took personal responsibility for his young teammate's sales success. At a meeting a month later, the team acknowledged this young fishmonger for his incredible growth, as his productivity was right with the top sales figures for the crew.

I emphasize to new hires that their personal success at Pike Place Fish and in their lives is completely dependent on their choices. I offer them the opportunity, but their level of commitment (consistently making choices that live the vision) will predict their success. Most of our guys come here with very little awareness of what true commitment means. They initially give lip service to making a commitment, but few of them know the rewards of living a life where you consistently choose, and are held accountable for choosing, to serve your team and your community. Once they make the commitment, they no longer just go along for the ride with me—they are actually driving. They begin to notice that the job becomes easier, and they create enjoyment in the job. They are not just going through the motions of doing the job; they are making a difference and creating joy for themselves. Some of the people we hire, like a relatively new crewmember, Matt, have an almost instant appreciation for the personal power and connection that come from living your commitments. He was like an athlete wanting to get in the game and play full out for the team, not for himself. I find that individuals change in different ways and on different timetables, and for many of our employees, the process of transformation is far less immediate.

Some people get the vision for a while and then lose their commitment to it. Their journey is a series of gains and setbacks. I have one employee who I thought would never work out. Over the course of his career with us, I have hired, fired, hired, fired, and hired him again. One time he was fired for drug problems. He came back with a commitment to change, sharing that he had cleaned up his drug addiction. When the team agreed to let him return, he started to lose his commitment to excellence by consistently showing up late for work. A year later, he came back again and asked for his job back. This time he looked and sounded different. He seemed to accept responsibility for himself in a different way, and the guys agreed to give him a chance to make the team again. The purpose of his life appeared to have shifted from pursuing his personal pleasure to giving something in service to others. He had grown personally and was up to living the vision of World Famous Pike Place Fish. He now takes responsibility for excellence and is an awesome teammate and a very empowering guy.

I find myself losing my commitment at times. I start making choices that aren't consistent with our vision. I get stuck in my anger, frustration, or desire to control other people's behavior. When my commitment wanes, Pike Place Fish is greatly affected. I am responsible for my choices, though, and fortunately, I always have the opportunity to instantly choose to bring my commitments alive in my actions.

It is often hard for new hires to understand the nature of the change they are facing when they come to work with me. After the first meeting, we routinely ask prospective employees, "How was the meeting for you?" In response, we often hear, "Pretty weird," or, "I have never been in a meeting like that before." Although it can sound exciting, it is difficult for a lot of people to realize that they have the power and responsibility to do more than sell fish. In fact, for some it's very difficult to grasp that they can personally make a world famous difference and create the success of our business.

Even if this idea seems strange in the beginning, Jim and I encourage all potential crewmembers to stay open to the possibility that they will fit with the vision. We ask them to take the time between meetings to observe other crewmembers as they go about making a world famous difference. Additionally, we ask the prospective employees to accept the feedback of the team and come to the next meeting with a willingness to explore further. Some people quickly understand what is being asked of them, while others don't. Some people go to one meeting and say, "Wow! This is not for me."

Throughout their first three months of pre-employment, new hires receive constant feedback from other team members. The team lets them know what's missing in their efforts to be world famous. Individuals who make a true commitment to the vision are willing to accept the feedback of their peers. By the three-month mark, the new hires have been supported by a team that coaches and holds them accountable for making a world famous difference. New crewmembers generally welcome this accountability, as it enhances their power to create success for the market. Often at the end of the three-month pre-employment period, new team members say things like, "You weren't kidding!

This is a huge responsibility," or, "I had no idea there is so much power in taking responsibility for myself."

After the orientation is completed, prospective employees announce their decisions to join the team by declaring their commitment to World Famous Pike Place Fish. This declaration is made in the presence of all other crewmembers and is an important rite of passage in our work community. It further increases our shared accountability to the vision. When a new staff member asserts that he has thoughtfully committed himself to World Famous Pike Place Fish, he invites his peers to support him as he makes the daily choices to create that vision.

OVERCOMING RESISTANCE TO CHANGE

At this point in Pike Place Fish's history, we are fortunate that our entire crew understands and lives the vision. This makes it easy to bring new people into our culture. It was very difficult, however, for our original crew to truly become World Famous Pike Place Fish. Although the concept of making a world famous difference emerged from that group, the process of learning to live the vision was slow and complicated.

Some of the early crewmembers had difficulty breaking old patterns of thinking and being. In fact, in the beginning, most of our team was ambivalent. They were both hopeful and cynical about our new path. I remember when I started bringing Jim to our meetings; the guys thought I was crazy. "Who is this guy sitting next to Johnny? Why does he keep telling us that we are responsible for creating a new opportunity?"

Prior to Jim helping us "commit to and be the vision," our

staff meetings were held on Saturday evenings near our office just outside the market. Most of the time, despite my best efforts, the meetings turned into complaint sessions. Frequently, the whining went into the late hours of the night. When Jim began his work with us, our first job was to change from being complainers and whiners to people who took individual responsibility for creating World Famous Pike Place Fish. Unfortunately, we had gotten rather comfortable with complaining and feeling powerless.

In our early meetings, guys drank beer and there was a lot of cussing and gossip. Over time, as a group, we agreed to stop drinking during the meetings, and even though it took five years, we agreed to stop smoking cigarettes during that time. We even made an agreement to stop swearing. That's a major accomplishment given that some of our staff are used to working on fishing boats. The dinner meetings evolved from a place to slam one another into an opportunity to coach and empower.

LISTENING AND SPEAKING RESPONSIBLY

An evolution occurred as Jim helped us emphasize the importance of taking responsibility for our own experience at Pike Place Fish. We spent a lot of time talking about the difference between blame and personal responsibility. This was a huge insight for a group of guys who had spent a lifetime seeing problems as occurring outside of themselves and believing that the solution to problems was someone else's responsibility.

As we made our transition, we asked our staff to start the meetings by sharing their upsets. We encouraged them to get their frustration out of their system. This, of course, was the easy part because that is exactly what they were used to doing. Then we forged an important agreement. Every crewmember accepted that before anyone spoke at the meeting, it was the responsibility of each listener to make it safe for anyone to say anything. This safe listening space was to be created even though what was being said might emotionally agitate the listener. Listeners knew that they could get upset about what was being said, but by agreement, they had to be quiet and just listen. Maybe the listener was experiencing nothing; maybe he was in total disagreement. In either case, it was the job of the listeners to take responsibility for their own reactions. In the beginning, it took a lot of practice, because the guys were used to hearing what someone said and "going off" in response.

When people fell back into old patterns and violated their agreement to create a safe listening space, we would bring the meeting to a halt and let the listener know that he had just broken the agreement. We would then remind him that regardless of what is said, the listener is responsible for refraining from speaking out. We would ask him if he could keep the agreement. On occasion, we actually had to ask a listener to leave because he could not maintain the integrity of his word. Although removal from the meeting might seem harsh, listeners were responsible for controlling their reactions. With that responsibility came consequences.

Through their shared commitment to create a safe listening space, listeners began to appreciate that as they listened, they attached emotional energy to the words of the speaker. The energy they gave to the words predicted how they would then react. We were exploring the idea that two people could hear the same words and make different choices in how they reacted to them. We were emphasizing that our crew could take control over their emotional reactions. It would take that type of control to make a world famous difference for angry customers or customers who had experienced a terrible day and took it out on a crewmember.

Ultimately, most of our original guys got the hang of creating a safe listening space and owning and controlling their own responses. They started to see the results of creating this safe listening space not only during our meetings but also in day-to-day interactions at work and home. Some of their reactions included, "When I listen to frustrated customers and I don't get defensive or argue, I notice my initial anger going away," or, "The more I listened and didn't make things worse, the sooner the other person felt like they could calm down."

Once the safe listening space had been created, our meetings focused on the responsibility of the speaker. We agreed that the person who was sharing the upset was also responsible for how it was shared. In the beginning, upsets typically were, "You did *this* to me and you did *that* to me." Given our new agreement, the speaker had to take responsibility for sharing the upset in a more constructive way—for example, "When you said that, I had this experience." No longer was the person who shared the upset able to present himself as the victim of another person's behavior. Through this process, the speaker learned to communicate in a less threatening way, saying something like, "I perceived you to do *this,* and I chose to feel *this* way. I want to communicate this because it is getting in my way of being an effective team member with you."

It is difficult for people to give up their righteousness and status as a victim and instead take responsibility for the way they express themselves at work. Ultimately, original crewmembers that chose to make the transition stayed on, and those who did not moved on. New hires become team members when they "get" that they are responsible not only for living up to their world famous commitment but also for listening and speaking in personally powerful ways.

| I I I |

Focusing on the Process
for Achieving Success

It's Not about the Fish,

It's about the Experience of Fishing

DISTINGUISHING BETWEEN DOING AND BEING

IT HAS BEEN SAID THAT MANY people go fishing their entire lives and never realize that it is not the fish that they are after. Rather than focusing on the journey of their lives, people often think only of arriving at a specific destination. The business philosophy of Pike Place Fish emphasizes the importance of the *journey* in each moment, focusing on each person we encounter in our work life.

To help fishmongers stay present with the moment-by-moment experience of their jobs and lives, Jim and I share a critical, yet seemingly complex, understanding about the notion of "doing" versus "being." Our guys have a pretty good idea of what it means to "do" something. Doing suggests planning and taking observable action. But our people often arrive on the job without a concept of "being." To them, "being" seems rather abstract. Being really is a definable concept. We help them appreciate that their way of being, in essence, is a reflection of their given intentions in a specific moment. If, while dealing with a customer or making a business decision, they intend to "be attentive to others' needs," then they are "being" considerate. However, if they act considerate while really intending to be self-serving, they are "doing" considerate but "being" self-serving.

In our case, fishmongers have committed to "be" World Famous Pike Place Fish; it is a very specific way of being. It means that they will operate at a high state of excellence in their physical work and be extremely attentive to people. Their job is to have an interest in customers and serve them no matter what. Even if customers are nasty with them, they need to "get over it." In fact, the game at Pike Place Fish is to see how quickly our staff can bring a smile to the face of a difficult customer. The game always is about the fishmonger choosing who he is "being" rather than trying to control events or other people.

ENCOURAGING SELF-MONITORING

Hundreds of times a day, I ask myself, "Who am I *being* right now?" I have committed to make a world famous difference at work and to *be* the best husband and father I can be at home. Am I being those things in this moment? If not, I can re-commit to those intentions and "be" those things. (Or I can choose not to "be," but at a cost.) For me, it is a matter of personal integrity. I don't have to plan how to "do" world famous things; rather it is a matter of clarifying my intentions and realigning my commitment to live those intentions.

Often, people aren't aware of their own intentions. It is human, however, to analyze the intentions of others. We try to understand others and react to them based on our own theory of why someone is acting in a certain manner. Often we feel that our personal power is limited by the intentions or behaviors of other people. We can see ourselves as having an inevitable reaction to the events that happen to us. We may even feel that we don't have the power to make choices because the people and situations at work do not let us. Classic examples of this occur when people say "He made me do it" or "What did you expect me to do when he said that to me?" By contrast, at Pike Place Fish, we work with our guys so that they understand they are generating their personal power in the space between their ears. Reality is shaped by who they are being, not by what others are doing to them.

Our guys are people of action. They want to make things happen. Like many Americans, our people often arrive on the job looking for the "way" to achieve results. They often think that they can make a world famous difference when they identify the specific behaviors or steps necessary to achieve it. As a society, we frequently look for "how-to" approaches instead of clarifying our intent, commitments, and way of being. Self-help books and radio-advice programs are constantly telling people how to do just about everything. Most of the time, advice is boiled down to seven easy secrets or four handy tips. While there is no shortage of books about how to achieve business success or how to lose weight, few people can turn this advice into wealth and thinness.

Being does not mean the absence of planning. It simply implies that you are not wedded to your plan; instead, you are committed to your intention. It means that you adopt a way to relate to the world instead of a specific course of action. Being is not about trying to control events in your life. Instead, it is about repeatedly choosing to stay the course of your commitments. It is a willingness to ask "Who do I want to be?" rather than "What should I do?" When you choose a way of being, the process begins, and the appropriate actions are rewarded moment by moment.

The discipline involved in *just being* is to refrain from over-strategizing. We all make short-term plans, such as what we want to accomplish during a presentation or how we want a vacation to go. But even in those situations, it is always a matter of making choices consistent with our intentions and then seeing what happens.

I am keenly aware of the challenge of living my intentions and not yielding the power of those intentions to the behavior of others. I often have to resist the temptation to try to plan my way out of difficulties in my life. A number of years ago, I shared a specific intention with my staff. I told them that I had committed myself to being a peacemaker and that I had a vision for world peace. My intention was to generate peace. You may think this grandiose, but given the effects of war on my childhood—my family and I were sent to live in Japanese American internment camps during World War II—and the continued ravages of war in the world, I felt it was important to take a stand for world peace. As is often the case, once you make a powerful declaration, you are given ample opportunities to test your commitment.

THE CHALLENGE OF LIVING YOUR COMMITMENTS

Shortly after declaring my intention as a peacemaker, a huge amount of turmoil began to surface at the market. Given the energy and notoriety of our fishmongers, they tend to draw large crowds around the shop. Their concern for people, attention to customers, and support of one another create rich, playful energy that is simply contagious. While it is good to increase foot traffic through the entire Pike Place Market, several neighboring merchants began to complain about the sprawl of people around our stand. When we first heard about these complaints, the crew and I reacted with, "You've got to be kidding! Don't they realize how we are a draw for people to pass by their businesses?" A couple of guys even talked about ways we could get back at the complainers. "If they think there are crowds here now, we can bring in even more if we only . . ." All of us, for a time, got hooked into *being* something other than peacemakers. We began choosing our actions based on the behaviors of the complaining merchants. Their complaints and not our intentions were running us. As we were being vengeful and self-centered, the situation worsened. In fact, petitions began to circulate throughout the market concerning the problem we posed to the flow of foot traffic.

One of our greatest critics was a man who owned a nearby Italian market. Several of our people noted that he would walk by our stand with a hostile scowl on his face. The reaction at our meetings in response to these reports was righteousness. "To heck with this guy. He's full of it. We generate business for him, and people come to the market to see us and he gets all this business." We actually spent time at a meeting thinking up strategies to fight the Italian market owner or counteract his attacks. For a time we were invested in our reaction and our strategies while ignoring our stated intentions. We lost sight of our commitment to World Famous Pike Place Fish and my vision of world peace. Finally, as a team, we reclaimed the power of living our commitments and regained our integrity. We had a meeting where we said, "Let's conclude that you guys are right and that the Italian market owner is a jerk. Do you want to be right about this, or do you want to be world famous? What would it look like to be world famous with him? Let's *be* world famous with the Italian market owner and create opportunities to make a difference in each moment with him." In one of those creative moments, a fishmonger suggested that Pike Place Fish could help the Italian market achieve greater success. With that world famous suggestion, a breakthrough occurred. What if we encouraged customers to stop by the Italian market when they needed items to complement their fish purchase? Suddenly, we created the opportunity to make a difference for the Italian market and enhance the lives of our customers as well. Instead of seeing the Italian market owner as a powerful force working against us, we were able to return to our intentions and create peacemaking options. As more customers went into the Italian market as a result of our referrals, the owner's complaints about overflowing traffic diminished and the petition movement ground to a halt. One morning, the owner of the Italian market actually said "hello" to one of our fishmongers; a few days later, he bought some fish! Thus, our people created the opportunity for a shared success to occur—not by planning or reacting emotionally, but by recommitting to *be* our vision!

LOOKING INWARD FOR PERSONAL POWER

In America, most of us are encouraged to act and to look for explanations for events that happen. We are typically taught that things that are true can be measured and explained. Our emphasis on seeking explanations and strategizing ways to do things is in itself neither good nor bad, but it is also not the only way to understand or relate to the world around us. For example, in some Eastern philosophies there is less focus on explanation and more emphasis on staying "present" with experiences. In these cultures, people are encouraged to move through life's pleasures and pains. Rather than seeking the one correct path, people are encouraged to become more in tune with the unique path they travel.

Jim and I share these alternative perspectives with my staff at Pike Place Fish. We encourage the team members to explore the possibility that they can be successful not by looking for a guru, mentor, or teacher, but by directing their attention inward to a state of being that generates personal power. We are not saying that mentors and teachers can't help you stay the course on your commitments and coach you back on your journey—certainly, Jim does those things for me—but that the answer to the question "How to?" may not be the Nike advertising slogan "Just Do It." Rather, its answer may best be stated, "Just *Be* It."

"Our deepest fear is not that we are inadequate. Our deepest fear is that we are powerful beyond measure. It is our light, not our darkness, that most frightens us. We ask ourselves who am I to be bright, brilliant, gorgeous, talented and fabulous? Actually, who are you not to be?"

—NELSON MANDELA

KNOWING WHETHER YOU'RE BEING
OR NOT BEING THE VISION

Maybe the best way to demonstrate our focus at Pike Place Fish is to share some examples of our crew *being* and *not being* world famous. When you're being world famous, you make big and small choices that make a difference for your coworkers and your customers. Some of the simple things include picking up after yourself so that coworkers do not need to do so on your behalf. Take responsibility for your messes, not because a policy manual tells you to, but because you are operating from a state of being that is committed to excellence and service to those who share your work environment.

On a slightly more significant level, one of my staff was *not* being the vision. He was distracted while offering free samples of salmon to passersby. He wasn't making eye contact with people as they approached. Rather than engaging guests in conversation, he was looking down with salmon samples in hand. Occasionally, the fishmonger would turn his back to the customers. One of his peers who was *being* the vision took the opportunity to make a difference for him by pointing to his own eyes and reminding his team member to look outside of himself. This subtle act of support came out of a willingness to help his peer make a world famous difference to the customers he was missing.

All of us go in and out of *being* the vision at Pike Place Fish. Our current staff makes great choices most of the time and offers great service to one another and to our customers. In fact, we get an overwhelming volume of phone calls, e-mails, and letters talking about what people have gained from their contact with us. Most of the time, the effect we have on customers is obvious and doesn't require follow-up documentation or proof. Recently, I saw a very stressed family walk by Pike Place Fish. It was a mother, father, and two small children. The family seemed tired. The kids were fidgety and the husband was telling his wife, "Just quit shopping and get to the car." As they approached the stand, one of our fishmongers greeted them warmly. He began playing with the children and taking an interest in the parents. He asked them whether they had had a busy day at the market, and he genuinely listened to the events of their day. When the woman asked about a particular fish, the fishmonger provided the information she desired. He asked where the family was from and whether they were buying the fish for a particular occasion, and he offered recipe and preparation tips. As my employee learned more about the people and made a personal connection with them, you could see the family relax and come together. The father picked up and held one of his children. He then grabbed his wife's hand while she kept her other child near. I don't know and don't care whether that family purchased fish that day, but I am certain that a small and important difference was created. My staff member was *being* World Famous Pike Place Fish, and he affected not only the family members but me as well. Who knows how this service to the family changed the course of their drive from the market, their dinner that night, their willingness to come back to the market in the future, or the way they shared the experience of the market with friends? The fishmonger treated the customers respectfully not to get a sale but because of his desire to make a difference. He was not using a sales technique or strategy. He was *being* of service, and he created a positive experience simply from that intention.

My staff understands what it means to be World Famous Pike Place Fish even when they are not physically on the job. For example, one of our fishmongers became aware of an article in *Newsweek* magazine written by David Noonan. The article, entitled "For the Littlest Patients," began this way:

> For 12-year-old cancer patient Christie Blackwood, the key to coping with chemotherapy was going back to "the place where they throw the fish." Christie was diagnosed with acute myelogenous leukemia in mid-September. Not unexpectedly, her initial chemo sessions were hard on the Minnesota seventh grader. "That first week was just hell," recalls her mother, Karla. "She didn't eat, and she vomited all week."

In the article, Christie talked about how she used her imagination to create a happy place to deal with the side effects of her treatment. Christie and her family used to live in Seattle, and her safe, pleasurable place was the Pike Place Market. Rather than simply reading about Christie with a mild interest, one of my crewmembers shared the article with one of his teammates and together they decided to bring the market ("where they throw the fish") to Christie in Minneapolis. When efforts to partner with an airline were unsuccessful, the two fishmongers shared their intention with me, and I picked up the tab on their airfare. At the end of Christie's thirteenth birthday party in the Minneapolis Chil-

dren's Hospital, a nurse on her unit announced "Here are the flying fish brothers" and in walked two World Famous Pike Place
Fishmongers. Respecting the sterile nature of the environment,
they brought new stuffed salmon pillows as an alternative to
actual salmon. Our guys threw these fish with Christie and other
young children on her unit. They left the stuffed fish, World
Famous Pike Place Fish T-shirts for all the children, and significant amounts of joy behind. At first, Christie was both delighted
and speechless. Her mother, Karla, noted, "I can't believe it, she
was so surprised and so excited. This was huge for her. It is unbelievable how these guys would travel all this way to do something
like this for someone they'd only read about." A nurse at Minneapolis Children's Hospital noted, "I have seen a lot of great
things happen in this hospital but this was exceptionally special.
The visit by the fish guys truly touched me. There is great kindness in this world."

Despite the crew's efforts to minimize publicity, a Minneapolis film crew had been told about the fishmongers' trip and
they produced a newsmagazine story that aired in Minnesota and
later in Seattle. A poignant moment in the news story occurred
when one of the two fishmongers on the trip became emotional
and started crying. This young man, age twenty-five, had under-
gone his share of health concerns dating back nine months earlier. He had developed a headache that wouldn't go away. He
went to his doctor and a CT scan confirmed that he had a golf-
ball-sized brain tumor that was inoperable. My staff member
underwent twenty-five days of radiation and three months of
chemotherapy. He shared his reaction and empathy for Christie
on camera by tearfully saying, "I know how hard it was for me to

go through it at my age, and to see these kids as young as five years old going through it, it was hard for me, and I can't imagine how hard it is for them. This trip did a lot for me, and it opened me up to making a difference for other hospitalized children in my area."

With only an intention to make a difference, my two staff members not only positively affected Christie and her family but the staff at the hospital and viewers in Minnesota and Seattle as well. We became very aware of how deeply this story affected people when a large number of visitors to the market came up and talked about it. Customers shared how they were "touched," "uplifted," and even "motivated to help others." Some Seattle residents told of phone calls they received from family members in Minnesota right after the news story aired there. People just came up and talked to us at the market about loved ones who had gone through cancer. Many visitors asked specifically for the "two fish guys who went to Minnesota" so they could thank them directly. Even our website had people thanking us: "We really enjoyed the video and seeing the guys doing their thing at the market. I was really impressed to see two of the Fish Market guys here in Minnesota visiting a thirteen-year-old girl with leukemia (it was her birthday wish). It was wonderful and tear-filled as the Fish Man spoke of his own brain tumor and began to cry seeing a little toddler awaiting his next chemo treatment for the same thing. (There was not a dry eye in our house.) It was great to see you guys living your philosophy . . . away from the job too. GREAT JOB, GUYS!" We have since learned that Christie is cured of cancer.

We have also had our share of disasters when it comes to

being world famous. One of our former staff members could never get the concept of being or making a world famous difference. He was too interested in being right about his negative assessments of people. His inability to put his own wishes, desires, and judgments aside in the service of others led to an episode where he actually yelled at a customer. That behavior was so out of line with our vision that our crew could no longer choose to have him on the team. We are all human beings and, as such, are subject to error. Some people, however, consistently choose to be something other than that which they have committed to. I believe that you can tell who you are being by the results that show up in your life. If anger and mistreatment of customers occur, you're not being world famous—you're being hostile, selfish, and uncaring. That fishmonger was not choosing to be or live his commitment to his team. His consistent and outrageous choices not to be a team member meant that he was choosing to lose his job.

GIVING STAFF OWNERSHIP

From my perspective as owner of Pike Place Fish, my most successful employees are those who live the vision the greatest percentage of the time. By being the vision, they learn their job duties quickly, accept the coaching of their peers, offer constructive feedback and support to their coworkers, master the technical skills of the job, provide exceptional customer service, take responsibility for themselves, and take risks to create new ways to be world famous. Their actions follow from their intention to make a world famous difference.

Let's face it—my staff serves customers all the time without me present. If they simply do what a procedure manual tells them, they will miss endless opportunities to bring their unique gifts and talents into the lives of other team members and customers. If they simply do things the way I want, they will be copies of me, and stifled, resentful ones at that.

Our people *are* all World Famous Pike Place Fish in their own way. I have guys who by their nature are rather gruff and direct; many have come from rugged experiences on docks and fishing boats. The way these guys engage and play with customers isn't something you would be exposed to in a class on customer service. I was watching an employee interact with a young couple the other day. The couple was standing back watching the fishmongers and other customers. My guy attentively noticed that the young man wanted to take his girlfriend's picture in front of the fish stand and that the young woman was somewhat reluctant. After gently establishing a rapport with the couple, the fishmonger asked the woman if she wanted to hold a large salmon for a photo. Our crewmember was present enough with her to realize that she had mixed feelings about the offer. There was a significant part of her that wanted to hold the fish, but her desire was overshadowed by her fear. Rather than gently say, "Well, that's okay, if you don't want to hold one, you don't have to," my employee picked a fish from the stand and began moving toward her with it. Her eyes were wide open and her hands were out in a somewhat fearful but partly accepting manner. As the woman started to back away, the fishmonger began to forcefully say, "Take it! Take it!" My employee was playing with the woman and encouraging her to overcome her fear and have a positive experience. She was beaming from ear to ear as she finally held the fish—at a great distance from her body, I might add. Her boyfriend, who was now also smiling, eagerly took her picture. No harm came to her, and she had been able to push past a mild personal limitation. She had made a connection with my employee, and they had all worked together to create a lasting photographic memory of the experience. By the way, the fishmonger did give her a towel to wipe her hands after the picture was taken.

There is no "how to" course that could or would teach someone to do what my crewmember did with the couple. The behavior he chose came out of his unique style and skills at *being* World Famous Pike Place Fish. He was not trying to act like me with those customers. I suspect I would have connected with them in a very different way. The fishmonger was being himself while being World Famous Pike Place Fish. Without effort, and operating from a pure and powerful intention, he made a difference. I am certain that, in this case, no fish were sold—but the picture will further the conversation about World Famous Pike Place Fish more than any advertising could.

LETTING POSITIVE INTENTIONS BE YOUR GUIDE

While we often think of "doing" as an active process and "being" a passive one, I find that creating an intention is very active and energizing. When I park my truck and walk to the market, I have a choice to either go in with a preset plan for how I will conduct my day or to go in simply as a person who will make the biggest difference he can. When I used to arrive with a set agenda, things were fine—as long as everyone and everything worked with my plan. When things got off course, there was hell to pay. I would wrestle for control and try to bring things back the way I knew "they should be." If things went off plan again, I would become righteous and complain or even yell at those people who interfered with my best efforts.

Nowadays, I believe that my positive intentions will guide me in the direction of success. As unexpected events and circumstances arise, I continue to strive to make a world famous difference. No matter what happens, I can still be a positive force for creativity and change. I need not, nor do I wish to, control the circumstances of the market. I simply need to *be* my commitment, and appropriate behaviors will follow.

If you are still skeptical, just be a positive intention for an hour. Choose any intention you wish. Maybe it's a matter of being the most attentive partner you can be or being the best parent possible. You don't have to figure out how you can "do" the attentive partner role or excellent parent hour. You don't need to read a book about improving communication with your partner or about more effective parenting. Don't pass go, don't collect $200. Declare your intention, don't exert effort on it—just *be* it—and your behaviors will follow from the intention. You will start a process that will increase your awareness of when you are being and when you are not being the intention. If you find you're not living your intention, you have an immediate opportunity to choose differently.

I notice that in situations where I feel that I have limited control, I am more likely to choose not to live my intention. When

Jim, the fishmongers, and I go out for a speaking engagement, I always work from the intention that we will make a great difference for the audience. This is a challenge when you are told that you will speak for a set amount of time after dinner only to find out that you will actually be speaking for a shorter time during dinner. In fact, we recently presented during a full-course meal where the audience not only was listening to us while eating but also was interrupted with the serving of wine, soup, salad, entrée, dessert, and then coffee. If I were to focus on the endless distractions or my expectations having not been met, it would not have changed how the dinner progressed. I would, however, have changed the person I was being as I spoke to the audience, and that would have reduced my power to make the difference I was there to make.

The experiences I have had in my own life and through the lives of my staff have reinforced the idea that as a supervisor, I no longer need to manage people. I simply need to coach them back to their most positive and powerful intentions. These days, I spend far less time telling people how to do things at work and more time exploring their intentions and commitments in each situation. I am most effective when I listen to them in a way that helps them look at their own way of being.

Through our intention to use World Famous Pike Place Fish as a way to serve other people, and the subsequent process that that declaration called forth, our crew has made a difference in people's lives and in the success of the market. We took on a way of relating to the world that has made an impact. We did not strategically set out a plan to bring ourselves fame. We didn't hire an ad agency to announce that we were world famous, call CNN, or do anything else of that sort. We simply committed to being world famous, and our actions followed from that intention.

Jim once noted the following so succinctly and clearly:

> Being is strategy in action. We don't make plans in the usual way. We create intentions and commit to them. We never know how the results are going to show up. So, while it's true that we've intended everything that has happened, the events seemed to come "out of the blue." Change really happens naturally, just out of who you're being. Our story is really a great testament to the power of commitment. People want to copy us— to do what we're doing. We keep telling them, your success isn't in doing what we do; it's in discovering your own way. Don't do what we do. You just have to be. That means commit yourself to being who you say you are: act like, think like, look like, feel like, and speak like. *Be* it! You will create your own way, and you'll create doing what you do. Our secret to success lies in our commitment to being who we say we are. Just be it.

| IV |

Changing Yourself First

Breaking Free from the Net

IT ALL STARTED WITH ME

NOTHING WOULD HAVE CHANGED AROUND HERE if I hadn't changed first. For many years, I was content to do things the way I always had. I was cynical and angry, and I didn't realize that unless I let go of those feelings, we were doomed. New and creative ideas were not of interest to me. Hard work and tried-and-true methods were what I thought produced results. My rigidity, burnout, and negativity kept us stuck. It wasn't until I re-created myself that a powerful vision to make a difference could appear. As I became more open to the ideas of my coworkers, our business began to achieve significant results and our vision was realized. It is amazing how many breakthrough ideas surfaced from the creative beings on my staff in support of our vision once I opened up to accepting those ideas. Take, for example, the introduction of computers to our workplace and the creation of our website.

I am not a very technologically inclined guy. If it were up to me, we would have never gotten computers at Pike Place Fish. It's not that I have any problems with computers—I've known that they have value, but I, personally, have had very little interest in them. One of my former managers became very excited about computers after having gotten one of his own. I would talk to him about that interest, mainly because I cared about him. He kept sharing with me ways in which the computer could help us at the market. At one point, he suggested that we get one. I asked him to let me know the cost and benefits of a computer, and then suggested bringing it up at a future staff meeting. While the decision would ultimately be mine, given the expense, I wanted to have the benefit of each team member's input. After our discussion, I told my manager to make the purchase. To be honest, I couldn't tell you much about that computer other than the fact that my computer-oriented manager was excited, but we started to notice immediate benefits. We began to get better control of our inventory and to organize our shipping. Prior to getting the computer, we were stuffing each month's shipping receipts into plastic bags.

As my manager saw more applications for computers, including automating our FedEx tracking system, we continued to stay open to his requests for additional computers, and now we have three computers in the work area alone. At one point, the manager came to me and suggested that we needed a website. While I personally would never have thought about the importance of such a thing, I encouraged him to once again research the idea and present it at a staff meeting. The team helped me appreciate the benefits of e-commerce, and I handed over $10,000 to a website designer and let my managers and the team create the site. That initial expense was not paid back in the first year, but we decided to revamp the website with an additional $10,000 investment. It took us four years before I could fully appreciate that the website was a good investment. Now, the website is an awesome vehicle for sales of Pike Place Fish worldwide.

The old me would have been grumpy and resistant to the idea of having a computer around. While not an excuse, that resistance, cynicism, and anger were a result of my early life experiences. My story begins in a Japanese American internment camp, but it ends with ownership of World Famous Pike Place Fish. It proves that everyone can make a contribution. There is nothing unusually special about me. I am truly an ordinary man. I have no exceptional talents. I never went to college. I have struggled with reading most of my life and really don't like to read much other than the sports page. I am proof that people are creative and powerful even without superior intelligence, exceptional business skills, or unusual luck. At times, when talking to audiences at business schools or major corporate conventions, I find it odd that as a high school graduate, I stand before these accomplished people to speak about business success. Then again, who else could tell the story of World Famous Pike Place Fish?

RECALLING THE PAST

My personal journey began June 25, 1940, in Seattle, Washington. I was the first of five children born to Roy and Helen

Yokoyama. My father immigrated to Seattle from Japan, whereas my mother, also of Japanese descent, was born in Seattle. On February 19, 1942, two months after the bombing of Pearl Harbor, our family was greatly affected when President Franklin D. Roosevelt signed Executive Order 9066. That order ultimately led to the nationwide incarceration of 110,000 Americans of Japanese ancestry. We were among those Americans. My mother, father, sister, and I were rounded up and taken to a processing center, the Tule Lake Relocation Camp, in Tule Lake, California.

Tule Lake was one of sixteen assembly centers where Japanese Americans were temporarily placed during World War II. At their high point, most centers housed between 3,000 and 7,000 evacuees. Usually, the centers were modified racetracks, fairgrounds, and livestock arenas. These locations were selected because they had built-in resources for water, electricity, and sewage.

Tule Lake was one of the most unsettled camps. It was common for prisoners there to hold protest demonstrations and strikes. Because of this, Tule Lake was made a "segregation camp" and was used to hold prisoners from other camps who refused to take the loyalty oath to the United States.

After arriving at an assembly center like Tule Lake, families were assigned to an "apartment." These apartments were often windowless rooms with partitioned walls and low ceilings. Because the rooms were often converted animal stalls, the odors of the prior animal residents remained. The "family apartment" was a space consisting of one room and was supposed to have cots, blankets, mattresses, a bare lightbulb, and a stove. However, there were often not enough of these supplies for everyone. Most prisoners left the assembly centers like Tule Lake in about 100 days and were sent to other camps.

I remember leaving Tule Lake on a long train ride to our next encampment, Minidoka Relocation Center in Hunt, Idaho. A sign at the present-day site of the Minidoka camp is fairly descriptive of our experience there:

> Victims of wartime hysteria, these people, two-thirds of whom were United States citizens, lived a bleak, humiliating life in tar paper barracks behind barbed wire and under armed guard.

In Minidoka, our family lived in a camp that was patrolled by guards and surrounded by barbed wire fences. It was divided into "blocks" consisting of twelve to fourteen barracks, a mess hall, bathroom facilities, a laundry, and a recreation hall. Each barrack was divided into four rooms, about twenty feet by sixteen feet. Generally, one room housed one family. I remember barracks being built from boards covered with tar paper.

We did not have running water at Minidoka. Water was available only at the laundry or bathrooms. Families ate together in the mess hall and bathed in community bathhouses. Food was a major issue in the camps. Mess halls were overcrowded. The meals were mostly dried fish, hot dogs, rice, macaroni, and pickled vegetables. It was a vast departure from what my mother would have prepared at home. There were shortages of meat and milk. Several camp administrators were accused of stealing food and selling it for personal profit.

Minidoka was a harsh place. Most of the employed internees

worked within the camps. They were used to clean or assist the camp administration. Many evacuees were given jobs to support the American war efforts. Other internees worked outside of the camps as contract laborers on local farms. My father was one of the contract laborers. One day while out working, my dad caught a jackrabbit and brought it home to me as a pet. This was the first time I remember my dad ever bringing me a gift. I was very excited about having a pet. That night, we kept him on the porch and tied him so that he wouldn't hop away. The next morning, I ran out to play with my rabbit, but it was gone. I went looking for it and was devastated when I found it being eaten by a dog.

Another example of the strain I felt at Minidoka occurred at Christmas. The camp officials kindly arranged a visit from Santa Claus. Unfortunately, I didn't know anything about Santa Claus. From my perspective, I was living in a place with all Japanese people when suddenly a large man with white hair and a white beard approached me. I dived under a table and hid there.

For a good portion of my life, I continued to hide. I hid inside the emotional wounds I sustained in the prison camps. These wounds were worsened by the treatment I received back in Seattle upon my return at age four. As if camp had not been difficult enough, our return to Seattle was even worse.

We lived in a housing project in Seattle upon our return from Minidoka until I was in junior high school. The other kids in the project would often call me and my family "dirty Japs" and "Jap bastards." I took their comments literally and thought they meant that I was unclean. This confused me, because I took a bath every day. I felt dirty, undesirable, and inferior to Caucasians. However, I do remember two occasions where Caucasians unexpectedly accepted me. When I was a kid in the projects, a white female store clerk called me "hon" when I was there buying a candy bar. It made me feel good. Later in life, while in high school, a popular Caucasian girl took a sip from my bottle of soda. It was striking to me that she would put her lips on a bottle where my lips had been.

Throughout my life, I was cautious in the way I acted around certain people. I didn't want to be called a "dirty Jap" anymore. I will never understand why people treated me so badly just because I was Japanese. But their words reinforced my feeling that as a Japanese person, I was less valuable than a Caucasian. Through much of my life, I feared what people were thinking of me.

By adulthood, I had become a very bitter and angry man. I justified my bitterness by saying, "How else could a person be, when at such a young age he was the target of such prejudice?" From the experiences I had at camp and the things that were said to me afterward, a deep inferiority complex was born.

PUTTING ADVERSITY IN PERSPECTIVE

The internment process had not only taken a toll on me personally and the Japanese American community in general, but it had also affected the Seattle Pike Place Market. The Pike Place Market is a nine-acre public market and historic district founded in 1907 on a vista above Seattle's southern, downtown Elliott Bay waterfront. In its present-day form, it is made up of more than 100 farmers, 150 craftspeople, nearly 300 commercial business-people, and countless street performers. A Seattle attraction, the market is rich with flowers, music, produce, crafts, and fish.

In the 1940s, the Japanese American internment stripped the market of many of its vendors. During and after the camp years, the Pike Place Market struggled. Most Japanese American farmers were forced to sell their property for a portion of its value with only a month's notice. Hundreds of the market's farmers were incarcerated in camps in Idaho. After World War II, the number of farmer-seller licenses plummeted from 515 in 1939 to just 53 in 1949. Upon returning to Seattle, my father was fortunate enough to be able to establish a produce stand at the Pike Place Market after working in another person's stand.

Although I was only an average student, my insecurities drove me to be a responsible and conscientious worker at my father's stand. My father's demands were for nothing short of perfection. He accepted no nonsense. If I did something wrong, I knew about it right away. If I upset him, I got whacked on the side of the head. Of all of the kids, I took the brunt of his strictness. Looking back from the context of that time, I wouldn't call my father's treatment of me abusive. In those days, that's how you raised kids. Unacceptable behavior resulted in being hit. As the oldest of five children, I was the example of what would happen if any of the others dared to misbehave.

On the positive side, my father helped me develop a great work ethic. He taught me to work hard and rapidly. From the time I was eight years old, I would take bunches of radishes and onions and split them into smaller bunches. My father would then sell these small groupings at three for a dime. I would rebunch ten crates of onions and ten crates of radishes (about ten dozen per box). That's a lot of radishes. When I finished the job, my father would reward me by letting me go to a movie. I figured out how to get the job done quickly. By contrast, my sister never got quick enough to make it to the shows.

Unlike children who enjoyed sports or other outside activities, I lived in a world consisting of school and work at my father's produce stand. The one great exception to those two activities was fishing! I've fished since I was eight years old. My fondest childhood memories are associated with fishing with my dad on Puget Sound. My love for fishing is likely due, in part, to my astrological sign of Cancer. My very being thrives out on the water. For me, fishing trips offered both peace and excitement.

My father and I fished for king salmon, although we also enjoyed catching silver salmon and, on alternating years, an incidental catch of pink salmon. We would get up at three o'clock in the morning and drive to Edmonds in northern Washington. Edmonds was, at that time, a small town with just a few homes, a restaurant, and a boathouse. My father owned a boat there, and we would bring the boat out and put it on a dolly. The dolly, which was on railroad tracks, would roll us into the water. We would fish two tides and wrap up by three or four o'clock in the afternoon. Those fishing trips were memorable times, as the fish were plentiful. If we didn't catch a fish within the first ten minutes, we were upset.

My father was relaxed out on the boat. He taught me everything I know about fishing. The first few times that we went out, he wouldn't trust me to land the fish. If I caught a big one, he would take the pole from me. One day, I had hooked a large salmon, and as he reeled it in, he lost the fish. I started crying. From that day on, my father never again took the pole away. He let me play my own fish.

We would fish virtually year-round when I was a child. I even remember times when it would be so cold that the salt water would freeze on the line as we brought it into the reel, or the water would freeze the windshield of the boat. Even in that weather, I was at home while fishing.

FINDING MY OWN PATH

My father expected me, the oldest son, to take over his business someday, but deep down I did not want that to be my future. One of the main reasons I disliked the job so much was the conflict I had with customers. In those days, we used to put up perfect displays. We would line up Brussels sprouts or cherries one at a time. This made for beautiful presentations, but unfortunately it also inspired customers to select their produce from the display. The problem was we didn't sell those items. When a customer made a purchase, we took their sprouts or cherries from a bin in the back of the stand and bagged them. A customer would often say, "I want the cherries from the display!" I would then have to tell them that I couldn't give them those cherries and that they would have to take the ones from the bins. When you created steady customers, they would trust you. But you were always dealing with new people. Customers were so used to going to a grocery store and picking out their own produce that it was a shock to them that they couldn't pick out what they took home. It was a different story at the nearby fish stand. People were less interested in touching and picking out their own fish. No one seemed to complain about having their fish handpicked for them.

I made a mental note as a kid that the fish business had fewer customer hassles than did the produce business.

As much as I did not like working at my father's produce stand, I expected that I was going to end up in the produce business anyway. As it turned out, my first real job upon graduating from high school was working at the Tradewell grocery store—where else but in the produce department. I had no vision for my future. I had no desire to go to college. Even if I had wanted to attend college, I wouldn't have had the opportunity. My father could not afford to send us. Produce was all I knew. It was my destiny.

After leaving the produce department at Tradewell, I started working at a wholesale produce company and came down to the market to help my dad. The owner of the fish market next to my father's produce stand asked me if I wanted a job. My passion for fishing had made fish a lifelong interest of mine. As a youth, while working at my father's stand, I watched intently as the fishmongers would fillet and skillfully cut fish. So here was my chance to jump ship from cherries and Brussels sprouts to fish. Why not? I took that job in 1960 at a fish market named Pike Place Fish. The very place I own today.

PURCHASING PIKE PLACE FISH

I worked at Pike Place Fish for a couple of years before spending three years at a wholesale fish company down on the waterfront. From these experiences, I learned both sides of the fish business—retail and wholesale. By 1965, I returned to Pike Place

Fish. At that time, I was one of several employees. The business had once been a thriving operation but by that point had turned hugely unsuccessful. Its failure occurred when the owner passed the business on to his son. The son, my boss, hated the fish business, and the business hated him. Given these problems, Pike Place Fish was put up for sale for $10,000. There were no takers. The price dropped to $5,000. Finally, the owner suggested that I take over the business. He knew I didn't have the money to buy it outright, so he offered me an unbelievable deal: $350 down and $300 per month, for a total of $3,500, and with no interest. At first I said no. As a young man of twenty-five, I was hesitant to take on the responsibility. However, the monthly payments on my new 1965 Buick Riviera were taking most of my paycheck, and I decided I could do better on an owner's salary. I went ahead and bought the company. You could say that I purchased Pike Place Fish to make my car payments! But this purchase was no easy feat, since $350 was my entire savings.

I remember asking my father whether I should buy Pike Place Fish. He had been in business at the market for a long time, and he knew I could make it. But how was I going to run the business when I had no cash reserves and no money for inventory? I went to all the wholesalers we had worked with and asked them whether they would give me thirty days' credit. Fortunately, all of the companies carried me for a month, and we had fish on the counter. It was a month-to-month proposition for a couple of years.

Over the next twenty years, I worked hard to make the business successful. Much of that time, I ruled my shop with an iron fist. My management style was essentially "my way or the highway," and many people took the highway because it was better than the alternative. Driven by self-doubt, my father's strict style, and a lifetime with my own share of hardships, I could unleash anger that made my employees—grown, burly men—cry.

Like my father, I expected perfection. It was the only way I knew to run the business. When someone made a mistake, I would get upset and start yelling and screaming. If an employee cut a fish wrong or wasted the product, I would be livid. One guy walked off the job right after I got through yelling at him. Of course when someone did that, I righteously thought, "All the better. If you can't take it, get out."

By the early 1980s, I was tired of carrying a huge chip on my shoulder, and I was certainly tired of carrying it alone. I enrolled in a series of personal development courses that helped me appreciate that there were other ways to treat people. Ways that involved enrolling others in decision making and taking responsibility for my own thoughts and feelings. These were novel ideas for me, and in many ways the courses helped me realize that I had manufactured a view of the world that had isolated me from the creativity of others. I had become unwilling to take chances, to trust others, and to venture out of my comfort zone. I had traded my capacity to love and embrace others for what I thought was security and safety. By examining myself and making new choices, I was able to be present with the possibility of making a world famous difference along with our team.

"Take your life in your own hands
and what happens? A terrible thing:
no one is to blame."

—ERICA JONG

Choosing Powerful Conversations

Removing the Hook

INCREASING PRODUCTIVE WORKPLACE CONVERSATIONS

IT IS DIFFICULT TO APPRECIATE HOW many conversations are taking place at work each day. If your workplace is anything like World Famous Pike Place Fish, there are conversations between your sales staff and customers, discussions among staff members, conversations with vendors, dialogue between managers, and communication between managers and those they supervise. No matter what the nature of the conversation is, it is essential to understand how some conversations are powerful and productive and others are limiting.

It is my belief that much of our success at Pike Place Fish can be directly linked to the commitment Jim Bergquist and I have made to help the staff distinguish between conversations that produce results and those that come up empty. This can take the form of conversations they have with one another or those swimming inside the head of each employee. In the case of private, internal conversations, we help employees bring their thoughts to the surface.

We serve as communication coaches, helping the staff determine that all conversations are not created equal. Some conversations support and empower people in their commitment to express themselves as world famous fishmongers. Other conversations distract staff members and take them down a path of upset, gossip, complaining, and mediocrity. Fortunately, every powerless conversation can be released so that a bountiful catch can be made.

GIVING PEOPLE SPACE TO SHOW UP DIFFERENTLY—MY STUPID LITTLE BROTHER DICKY

He's always been "my stupid little brother Dicky." For the first fifty-seven years of my life, he was stupid. He was the one who started smoking young, wrecked my dad's car, wrecked his own car, took off for California with a bunch of his buddies without telling anybody—my dad had to go get him. He generally acted far less responsibly than I did—*stupid*! Lucky for me, my stupid little brother Dicky couldn't create much trouble working for me behind the counter at Pike Place Fish.

When I asked my retiring store manager to suggest a replacement manager, you can imagine my surprise when he uttered my brother's name. I must have misunderstood him. He could not possibly think my stupid little brother Dicky could take over for him. "Come on! This is *Dicky!*"

As my old manager was leaving Pike Place Fish, he convinced me to give Dicky a chance. Against my better judgment, I promoted my brother to manager. The whole time, my internal conversation concerning his incompetence plagued me. It also led me into many other disempowered conversations, such as, "I have worked all these years to get to a state of semiretirement, and Dicky is going to ruin it all." Or, "I'm going to have to be at the market full-time, or my stupid little brother will run the market into the ground." These conversations shaped my attitude and behavior. I started going to the market more consistently and, as expected, I saw endless mistakes being made. The cash receipts would not balance at the end of the day, reordering was slow, there was no sense of urgency, and profits were declining. What did I expect? After all, *Dicky* was the manager!

One day, while I was discussing the situation with Jim Bergquist, he asked me to look at the internal conversation I was having about my brother and how it shaped my willingness to both support and acknowledge him. My conversation about my stupid little brother Dicky was based on a lifetime of experience. It boxed both of us into the past, limited our relationship, and restricted his ability to flourish as manager. Could I adopt an alternate conversation? Could I start seeing my brother as a great manager? What about my investment in being the smarter, righteous older brother?

When I first began talking to Jim about choosing a different conversation about Dicky, he helped me explore my willingness to see Dicky as the best manager Pike Place Fish had ever had. At one point, I told Jim that I could choose to see Dicky in that way. But even though I was open to that interpretation, I really had not committed to letting go of viewing him as a screwup. At first, I was hoping Dicky would be a more competent manager, but I hadn't changed the way I related to him, and our relationship didn't really change. You could say that I was *trying* to change. But there really is no state of being called "trying." For example, let's take picking up a fork. There are two states of being in the process: the state of having not picked it up and the state of having picked it up. There is no point in the process you can define as having tried to pick it up. Trying to pick it up is the same as not picking it up. Intellectually, I understood that I had boxed my brother in by the way I thought about him and the way those thoughts affected who I was being with him. I just had not "picked up" the state of being that gave Dicky space to be the best manager we had ever had. I finally chose the more powerful conversation about Dicky's greatness when I declared it at a staff meeting and started being a person who didn't make Dicky wrong.

How quickly things changed! As Dicky had more space to become a success, received less criticism for mistakes, and was offered more assistance with problem solving, he emerged as a world-class manager. His leadership has guided Pike Place Fish to record productivity, despite inheriting one of the least experienced crews in Pike Place Fish history. He eclipsed sales records I thought would never be duplicated. His praises are sung regularly. It is not unusual to hear crewmembers acknowledge him as the "best manager we have ever had," or as a man who treats them with respect and "pushes us to be our best." The best manager for Pike Place Fish has shown up—and he is my brother Dicky. And that's saying a lot, because *I* once was the manager of the company.

Each of us participates in internal dialogues. Much of this self-talk prevents us, and the people that work with us, from realizing our full potential. Some of the most power-limiting internal conversations we encounter at Pike Place Fish are probably occurring in your workplace as well. One classic example of "disempowered" speech is the blame game.

TAKING RESPONSIBILITY FOR YOURSELF

About a year ago, one of our newer crewmembers assumed expanded responsibilities that included picking up fish from our wholesaler at the waterfront. One day, while stopping at the market, I noticed that the quality of some of our fish on display was below our world famous commitment. As I explored it further, I found out which staff member had picked up that particular shipment. When I approached the fishmonger and asked whether I could coach him about picking up shipments, he said, "I know this isn't up to our quality, boss, but I felt pressured by the wholesaler to take the fish." I invited him to look at the internal conversation he had had about what it meant to be World Famous Pike Place Fish when he was picking up the order. My crewmember said, "I told myself that I didn't have a choice, because if I turned down the shipment, it would take a long time for the wholesaler to fill the order with better-quality fish. I would have been away from the market for too long."

I realized that I had not provided enough coaching to this

young fishmonger before he began picking up deliveries. I encouraged him to explore his power to say no anytime he's picking up a shipment when the quality does not meet our world famous standards. He then understood that if he took a stand for quality, his teammates would support him through their commitment to our vision. In talking to him later, he thanked me for the opportunity to learn and noted that in previous jobs his choice would have been looked at as a mistake. According to him, his previous managers would have typically tried to lay the blame on someone. From my perspective, blame has no purpose, and it is a lousy teacher. The situation we had with the quality of fish on the stand that day was the result of many different factors. All of us had to look at the portion we contributed to the problem so that a creative solution could occur. For example, my fishmonger's coworkers and I took responsibility for not having adequately coached him on the importance of quality assurance when picking up fish. We hadn't communicated clearly to our young staff member the downside of accepting an inferior product: namely, that either our customers would be getting an inferior product, or we would be unable to sell it. The team and I had the power to be better and to assist our teammate in his pursuit of our vision.

The issue concerning fish quality gave us all an opportunity to explore what each of us could do to maintain our continued and shared commitment to making a difference in people's lives at the market. Our young crewmember was not a victim of the wholesalers. His experience led to an opportunity for growth. Since that experience, he has empowered himself by employing a more effective conversation. He chooses that conversation each time he brings back awesome fish. That fishmonger has become known as the "quality-control guy" for the market, because he made such a powerful shift in his conversation about what he will accept in the name of World Famous Pike Place Fish.

BY CHANGING YOUR CONVERSATION, YOU CHANGE REALITY

Although our fishmongers shift conversations from blaming to taking personal responsibility almost daily, one of my favorite examples occurred during the Christmas rush at a time when we had a rather inexperienced crew. We were really busy packing shipping orders. I was working out front and one of my veteran employees was really upset. He came over to me and said, "I need to talk to you. These guys don't have a clue what they are doing. We're in big trouble—everything is really messed up! This crew sucks; they don't know what they're doing!" I said, "Stop! What's the conversation you're having with yourself right now? Listen to the conversation that's shaping you." He immediately said, "I got it." I asked, "What can you create as a new conversation for yourself?" I could tell that at that exact moment he decided to change who he was being with the crew. The conversation he chose was, "We are a great crew. Things from this point on will go smoothly and excellently."

I saw my employee change dramatically as he changed his conversation. When he went back behind the counter, the entire environment altered. Everything improved. The orders got packed quickly and efficiently. That day, and the entire week, went by without a hitch, and we had record sales. If you get attached to a conversation that says all of the people around you are incompetent, it's likely that you will try to do everything by yourself. When you shift conversations and explore the greatness of your team members, you're likely to be a person who creates opportunities for their strengths to show up on the job. Sometimes it's not about "doing" more, it's about choosing a conversation that empowers you to make more of a difference.

GETTING RID OF GOSSIP

In a world famous organization, there is no room for gossip. It is a destructive force and reflects a way of being that undermines other people in the workplace. Even listening to gossip creates a hostile environment and severely limits a person's ability to make a difference for coworkers. While we have talked a great deal about this danger in our staff meetings, we are human beings, and occasionally we have to revisit the power-limiting aspects of sharing or receiving gossip.

We once had an employee who had just not gotten our vision. His lack of commitment to the vision could be seen in how slow he was in getting the fish show set up and in a general lack of pride in his work. Several fishmongers voiced complaints about him to a manager. This prompted the manager to help the guys take this intense *negative* energy and channel it into an opportunity for growth. At a staff meeting, the manager shared, "Hey guys, lately lots of you have been coming to me complaining about this individual. Let's take a look at who we are being when it comes to him. Who wants to take responsibility for gos-

"Without knowing the force of words, it is impossible to know men."

—CONFUCIUS

siping and complaining?" Several fishmongers acknowledged that they had been talking to the manager and others rather than going directly to their teammate, while other fishmongers acknowledged that they had been listening to those criticisms. Given that these team members had reached this point of acknowledgment, we asked them, "Where do we go from here?" Individually, the fishmongers committed to directly coach their crewmember and to not participate in negative conversations about him. One fishmonger in particular took the additional step of sharing directly with his teammate several specific things that were upsetting him. The two fishmongers cleared the tension between them, and the target of the gossip saw how his prior resistance to accepting coaching contributed to the gossip about him. He strengthened his ability to be a team player, giving him a greater sense of our vision.

AVOIDING ON-THE-JOB LAPSES

In many of the examples I am sharing, someone encourages awareness of a power-limiting conversation that is going on. As you become more in touch with the types of conversations that limit your power, you can catch yourself and make a more powerful choice. Take one employee of mine who was behind the counter and was not delivering particularly world famous customer service one morning. In fact, he was having an internal conversation that went something like this: "I don't want to be here this morning. Oh no, here comes a customer. If I act like I am busy, maybe he will go away." By indulging that conversation, he was choosing to let his feeling of "not wanting to be bothered" get in the way of the commitment he had made to himself and his coworkers. The customer did not go away. In fact, he attempted to get my staff member's attention. The staff member reportedly became more frustrated and more deeply indulged his conversation. "Geez! What is with this guy? I don't want to go down to the other end of the fish stand. He probably isn't even going to buy anything anyway." The employee didn't have to walk to the end of the fish stand, because by this time the persistent customer was approaching him. As the customer came forward, my team member apparently realized how his conversation had taken him away from his commitment to making a world famous difference for this customer. Without the assistance of anyone else, he simply chose to shift the conversation and retain his power to live the vision. It turned out that my fishmonger made a huge sale, but more important, he made a connection with this customer, who as it turned out was the manager of several of this guy's favorite music groups. The customer gave the fishmonger backstage passes to a favorite band's concerts.

PUSHING PAST COMFORT ZONES

At times, we all miss opportunities to use our personal power at work. Sometimes, we're just not in a good mood, or we don't feel like investing the energy to make a difference. In my case, I frequently "just don't want to" do what it takes to get out of my comfort zone. My basic personality is anchored to resisting new opportunities and situations. Frankly, I often find myself "not wanting" to do things that I know I would enjoy if I could just get myself out of my house. For example, I'll make plans to do something in the future. It is typically something that sounds fun. However, when the time arrives to actually go to the event, I dread having to go. I suspect this automatic conversation has been a part of me from my formative years. Who knows? Maybe my mother had a difficult time with my birth because I just didn't want to face the world, even then. Being aware of our power-limiting conversations and sharing them with people who support us can help ease the transition to more powerful discussions.

Jim Bergquist and my wife, Diane, are quick to anticipate my "I don't want to" approach to work and life. They began conspiring together when we were asked to consult internationally for the first time. Both of them knew my basic nature and my specific dislike for travel, let alone international travel. From the moment the opportunity was offered to me, I began to bristle. "Why would I want to go there? I didn't lose anything in Scotland. If they want to consult with us they can come here."

These conversations were just the tip of a large iceberg centered on my core internal conversation. I didn't want to experience personal discomfort. I did not want to go outside of the environment I had crafted for myself in Seattle. Jim and Diane quickly helped me get over it. Among other things, Jim pointed out that my conversation would limit my ability to ever play St. Andrews golf course and to live up to my commitment of being *world* famous, unless my world was restricted to Seattle. Diane simply said, "Come on, Johnny! Go out and make a difference today." Jim and I did make a difference, on and off the links in that beautiful part of the world. Experiencing the power of making it through that trip has made it easier to travel to other parts of this diverse planet.

LETTING GO OF FEAR

Diane knows a great deal about my automatic conversations. She has been dealing with them since even before we married in 1982. In fact, it took me getting past one of those conversations for us to be together at all. I had been married before, back in 1965. It was around the time I purchased the market. That marriage lasted only one year, as my first wife became involved with another man. The divorce completely devastated me because I believed that you married for life. After my divorce, I had a running internal conversation telling myself I couldn't trust women. I had terrific relationships with wonderful women, but invariably my fears about women seemed to be realized. My actions would cause an incident in a relationship, and then I'd use the incident to justify my fear. My fears created no space for me to trust women.

Despite my constant failures with women, I didn't stop trying. In fact, it was through an effort to impress a woman that I found myself going to an orientation for a personal growth course. There was a woman who was working across the street from us. She was a flight attendant, and her airline was actually on strike at the time. I really wanted to take her out. I knew she was interested in this personal development seminar, and given that I was looking for a change in my life, I asked her whether she wanted to go to an information meeting with me. She said yes, so I went with her and she enrolled in the full program. It was about a week after that that she was going to go back to the airline, and I feared I might not see her again, so I enrolled, too. Although I did not marry the flight attendant, taking the course allowed me to change some of my automatic conversations, which resulted in my future wife, Diane, wanting to go out with me on a second date.

I had met Diane on the waterfront a number of years earlier. She used to work for one of the wholesalers from whom I bought fish. It had been some time from when I had met her to when we actually had our first date. On that date, we took the hydrofoil up to Vancouver. I hated everything on the date. I hated the window shopping, the food, everything. All I did was complain. To hear her tell it today, Diane could hardly get off the hydrofoil soon enough to get away from me. We did not date much after that until I began changing some of my automatic conversations. These changes included letting go of negative and complaining internal and external conversations. As I changed my conversations to more powerful and constructive ones, I became more attractive to Diane. Reciprocally, Diane's support and strength have served to help me effectively choose more powerful conversations each day.

What conversations are automatic for you? How do you and those with whom you work yield to power-limiting conversations? By stopping automatic, passive, and power-reducing conversations we unleash dynamic and generative forces that drive our success and fuel our ability to make a difference. Creating deep and powerful conversations works for us at Pike Place Fish, and powerful conversations have positively transformed the lives of our families as well.

Making a Difference by Listening Intently

Hush, or the Fish Won't Bite

LISTENING—ON AND OFF THE JOB

I'D JUST FINISHED A PRESENTATION, AND the audience seemed to truly appreciate my message. It was obvious from the reaction of the listeners that people were beginning to explore new possibilities in their business and personal lives. As I boarded the plane for the four-hour flight back to Seattle, I was ready to sit back, relax, and frankly, be left alone. When I took my seat, a skinny, rather unattractive, poorly dressed woman sat down next to me. To be quite honest, she looked like a homeless person. My first thought was, "How could she possibly have paid for the ticket for this flight?" I was hoping she wouldn't talk to me, because there was no way we would have anything in common. How quickly I had shifted from being a person committed to making a difference during the presentation to someone who wanted to keep to himself and pass judgment on other people's appearance.

My desire for solitude was challenged when the woman began to talk to me. As I was about to give her a courteous response designed to shut down further conversation, I caught myself and asked, "Who am I going to be now? Am I going to be a person who shuts her out? Or will I listen to make a difference?" I am glad I chose to listen. What an awesome and powerful opportunity I was given.

My thoughts about my traveling companion changed quickly once I got to know her. Despite prejudging her to be poor and likely uneducated, it turned out she was, of all things, a physician. As we talked, the conversation became increasingly rich and meaningful. At one point, she shared her dating history and the problems she had encountered because of her beliefs about remaining a virgin. A woman I had initially judged as unattractive and homeless was actually an exceptional, beautiful person with deep convictions. By listening for the chance to make a difference, we connected and she shared both the excitement and the loneliness of her life. I felt honored that she would tell me so much about herself. I was genuinely fascinated by her story. I pushed past the way I normally act on a plane and didn't even try to watch the in-flight movie. By being different in the way I listened, I had experienced one of the most enjoyable airplane rides of my life. I was glad that I hadn't missed the opportunity to come to know her. At the end of our travel together, we shared contact information. Some days later, she sent me a thank-you note and a booklet about her faith. To think that she wrote and thanked me—simply for taking an interest in her.

LEADING THROUGH LISTENING

While I don't always appreciate the power I have to make a difference in the course of my daily travels, I know that when I listen to people it opens up opportunities and possibilities. This is particularly obvious and essential when it comes to listening to my staff. If I am not listening actively to my crew, I fail to create the environment where they will listen to one another and to our customers. If I don't listen to the needs and concerns of my staff, I can't reasonably expect them to listen to those same needs of their team members and our customers. My behavior sets the tone for our company.

Our customers come to us with their own issues and desires. Some show up at the market simply to watch us, others come to buy a pound of shrimp, and yet others want to create an awesome party. It is our job to listen for the customers' needs, and sometimes help the customers clarify their desires, but ultimately to serve them and make a difference for them in that process. Before my employees can provide any of those services, however, their own needs and concerns must be honored. That's my job as the owner. I choose to know and care for them.

Go into a business and ask the manager questions about her team: "How many kids does that employee have?" "How old are his kids?" "What's the biggest challenge in that employee's life?" "What does that person love to do on weekends?" Some managers, sadly, will tell you that they don't know many of these answers and, furthermore, don't care to know them. From their perspective, that's "personal stuff, not work-related information." Come on! My employees are people first and fishmongers second. Personal and work-related issues are all the same to me. I want to know what's going on with our crew. My openness springs from a genuine interest in their lives. I know that my care for them (I am comfortable calling it love) is vital as they create a listening space for one another and for our customers.

When a new employee makes the team, I personally commit to make a difference for that person—not only to help him be the greatest fishmonger he can be but also to help him have a great life. Some managers may think I am crazy. Should there really be a commitment to staff members beyond creating a positive work environment? My employees are not "human resources"; they are people. I can actually remember a time when I thought, "Who cares what kind of life my crewmembers have as long as they produce at work." I can no longer see team members as human resources similar to computers, paper products, and other supplies. My staff is made up of very special people. Each one of them has a unique creativity as well as individual needs and abilities. The choices I make assisting my employees to "have a great life" may seem strange to some people, but those choices fit my commitment to World Famous Pike Place Fish and a way of being that works best in my life.

"When we are listened to, it creates us, makes us unfold and expand. Ideas actually grow within us and come to life."

—BRENDA UELAND

INVESTING IN YOUR STAFF'S WELFARE

It doesn't take effort to love your people. In fact, I would argue that it takes effort not to love them. Sometimes, it is as simple as just listening to my employees. I don't need to fix their life concerns but just be a person who takes an interest and actively listens to them. Just as parents want their teenagers to feel comfortable with them and share any problems that arise, I want to be the kind of listener that invites employees to share their personal and work concerns. Recently, a crewmember stopped me and asked if we could talk. It turned out that he was having a conflict with a roommate, and he wanted my feedback. In reality, I said very little. I just listened. I knew that I couldn't change his roommate. Because I supported him with listening and encouragement, he took responsibility for his part in the dispute and chose to make a positive change in the way he was being with his roommate. His anger toward his roommate softened as he talked, and he appeared more peaceful and confident in his ability to generate change in the situation. I'm not sure who benefited more from our discussion. What he gained was matched by the reward I received from being trusted to listen to his upset.

In other situations, listening to employees and being present with them results in my taking additional action to support them. For example, one of my guys started working part-time on weekends when he was fourteen. After years of loyal service, he noted, "I've been working here six days a week, this is all I've ever done. It's all I've ever known, and what do I have to show for it? I want to buy a house." He asked me for a loan and I gave it to him. Since then, he has not only repaid the loan but gone well beyond the call of duty through his incredible service to Pike Place Fish and our customers.

Another longtime employee moved to New York. After working in a fish department at a supermarket there, he was eager to come back to Pike Place Fish. His only reluctance was that he did not want to commit to a fifty-two-hour workweek. He told me, "I love working at Pike Place Fish, but I can't devote twelve hours a day, four or five days a week, to being a fishmonger. If I spend that much time at the market, I can't pursue my music career. When I work so many hours, I'm not as sharp in the music studio, and I want my music career to be a success." I listened intently and simply asked, "What days do you want to work?" I made him responsible for working out the details with the rest of the team. He also let me know that he needed health benefits, although he would only be part-time. That was not a problem.

In the old days, I would have never let an employee "get away with" special treatment or a request to be treated differently than the rest of the team. But with my personal evolution and commitment to employees, I want each crewmember to know that if something is wrong at work or at home they can come to me. That doesn't mean that I can or will take action on every issue they raise. Frankly, I can't afford to say yes to all my staff's desires, but one thing is certain—I can't afford the outrageous cost of not listening to their requests.

CARING DESPITE DISAPPOINTMENTS AND BETRAYALS

Many people think that crossing into the personal life of employees is a huge mistake. I understand how they could see it that way. Managers from other businesses have told me that they used to take an interest in the lives of their employees until they were "ripped off." It is as if these managers stopped listening for ways to improve the quality of their employees' lives because of some past wound. I can assure you, I know the pain of having my trust violated.

I have been taken advantage of more times than I care to recall. Sometimes it has been through theft or embezzlement, but the worst situation was when a former employee sued me. I had consistently worked with this particular fishmonger so that he could succeed at Pike Place Fish. It was a constant challenge as he struggled to live our vision. When he was on, he was terrific. When he wasn't on, he was a disaster. The entire team took care of him, even when he was at his most difficult. After he'd had seemingly endless chances, his lack of commitment cost him his place on the team, and I let him go. Rather than appreciating all the effort that we had invested in him, he filed a lawsuit against me. Worse yet, he looked for other former employees and attempted to get them to sue me as well. His legal issue was my payroll practice. At the time, I paid all my employees a salary. I also offered my crew incentives based on the profits we collectively earned. Back in those days, my employees worked sixty hours per week, so my disgruntled employee sued me for unpaid overtime. He won, and I was hurt—both emotionally and, to a lesser degree, financially.

At that point, no one in the market paid overtime, so I could have justified my mistake the way a kid would, saying, "Why do I get in trouble when all the other kids are doing the same thing?" Holding on to that conversation would have kept me stuck as a victim. I had assumed that a base salary with profit incentives was okay. I learned from that lawsuit that I could pay salaries only to my managers. It was my mistake, and I took responsibility for it. At first, my reaction to the entire lawsuit was one of sadness and betrayal. Initially, I thought, "Man, I was burned!" I wondered if I could ever make myself that vulnerable to my employees again. Finally, after much painful consideration, I asked myself, "Who am I going to be now? Am I going to be someone who doesn't trust his crew, or am I going to leave the opportunity open for employees to be trusted?" Personally, I decided it is better to trust, because that fits my life better.

CREATING AN ENVIRONMENT FOR PEOPLE TO HAVE GREAT LIVES

My commitment to my employees is to make their lives great. There are no "ifs, ands, or buts" about it. I have taken a stand to support all of my employees as they create whatever they view to be a great life. My commitment is not to support them "only if" their view of a great life agrees with mine. They create their own vision of greatness, and I help them embrace that vision.

For some of my people, a great life means leaving Pike Place

Fish to go somewhere else and create new opportunities. When that happens, I help that employee make the transition. While my central job is to make a difference for each of my people right now—while they are employed at Pike Place Fish—I realize that whatever they learn while they are with me will be taken along with them. Once an employee has realized that he has the power to make a difference in the lives of others, his commitment to service goes well beyond the confines of my fish market and well beyond the time I employ him.

A guy who worked for me for quite a long time was always committed to growing and making a difference. While working at the market, he attended college. He completed his bachelor's degree and went on to finish a master's degree. The time came for him to leave Pike Place Fish and I was sad to see him go. My sadness gave way to delight as he took a job in his area of study and became a high school teacher. I knew he would make a huge difference to many students and to his own five children. It's gratifying to see him continue to occasionally attend our staff meetings. He told me that he continues to share his experiences from Pike Place Fish as he works to make positive changes in the educational system.

DEALING WITH DIFFICULT EMPLOYEES

While I enjoy listening and paying attention to my staff, I occasionally run across a person I have a difficult time connecting with. I once had an employee that I had a bad feeling about from the beginning. Sure enough, that crewmember lived down to my expectations. Every time I was around him, I would get upset and stop listening to him. It seemed to me that whenever he opened his mouth, he was complaining about being a victim of one circumstance or another, and he just didn't want to take responsibility for himself. It got to a point where I just didn't want to hear what he had to say. My ears were closed as far as he was concerned. I saw him as hurting business and having a negative effect on the team. Sometimes, I would just see the look on his face and I would tune him out. I missed many opportunities to connect with him, and I am sure that my reaction to him in turn affected the way he felt about me. Somewhere along the way, I realized that if I ever needed to listen to someone, it was to that fishmonger. There was no way we were going to achieve a workable relationship unless I created an opening for him. I chose to listen for ways that he and I could get over the attitudes we had developed about each other. I took an interest in him instead of looking the other way. I had to shift from being someone who didn't want to deal with him and return to my commitment to make his life great. I wanted to support him at work and beyond. It was never easy for us, but from that point forward a constructive relationship began.

The commitment to listening and creating opportunities for crewmembers' growth shows up in many ways. On various occasions it has meant supporting staff as they get off drugs or alcohol. I have chosen to bail crewmembers out of jail when they've gotten into domestic disputes during ugly divorce battles. My commitment has been demonstrated in as many ways as my people have had needs. From my experience, I am certain that owners and managers can create an environment where their employees listen differently to one another and to their managers.

TEACHING A TEAM TO LISTEN

When staff members feel that their manager listens to them, they are more likely to extend the benefits of listening to their coworkers. Listening gives people access to their creativity and assists them in relating to one another. In the beginning of most relationships, there is underlying tension. People often are concerned about what other people think of them. They wonder, "Will I fit in?" "Am I going to look good?" "Am I interesting?" "Will I be accepted?" This nervous uncertainty is going on with people all the time, and it can greatly affect how well people work together as a team. If you are thinking about how your teammates view you, your attention is focused on your own thoughts and not on the needs of the team. All the worry happening inside your head is not the result of what other team members are doing or thinking. It's what you are creating and who you are being. When a coworker comes up and offers constructive feedback on how you can make a greater difference, you choose between listening to benefit from that person's input or listening to hear how you "screwed up." Getting lost in ourselves and listening to our own interpretations of the world often gets in the way of taking charge of our lives.

In many jobs, people get feedback from a boss or coworker, but they don't listen to see whether there is something in the feedback that can help them as they grow. Instead, they listen with defensiveness. People look for ways to make the feedback wrong, or they try to defend themselves from what they hear as criticism. Listening for helpful advice means creating a new interpretation where you can hear lessons rather than attacks. Individuals make the choice as to how they interpret the advice. Looking for a lesson means that you embrace your personal power to search for something constructive while at the same time yielding your own need to be right or to justify yourself.

When we fear what other people think about us, we are frequently more focused on "being interesting" and less focused on "taking an interest." That's why many people talk a great deal when they are anxious and why many people never feel heard. If both people in a conversation are trying to be interesting, there is no one left to genuinely listen.

Jim and I help the team look at "who they are being" when it comes to staying open to opportunities and taking an interest in others. While the guys generally do a great job focusing on the needs of customers, they are human beings and can get distracted by television cameras or by people they find attractive. It is during these distractions that you can see the staff hold each other accountable for taking an interest in the customer that is in front of them instead of "looking interesting." A film crew was shooting a commercial down at the market when I heard one fishmonger say to another, "Let's get back to making a difference, Hollywood."

On busy days, we draw large crowds of onlookers and customers. When there are a lot of people stopping by to watch the fishmongers, it's easy for my crew to get swept into entertainment mode. The intense laughter and reactions of the crowd can be intoxicating. Customers regularly ask our guys for their autographs, request that they pose in pictures, and generally wait to see the fishmongers do something interesting. These crowds offer the team ego-boosting attention, and occasionally one of my guys gets hooked by his own sense of self-importance. When I see a fishmonger looking or acting as though he thinks he is a celebrity, I simply ask, "Are you being famous? Or are you being someone who is making a world famous difference?" The crew knows this distinction well. They are able to explore who they are being and to take themselves out of the limelight and shift their focus back to the customers.

When you live your life with a genuine interest and concern for others, it is clear when members of your team aren't listening to make a difference. It is easy to coach them and receive coaching from them to make sure that they are listening to one another and to those who come into contact with your business.

CUSTOMER SERVICE *IS* LISTENING

I see employees at other workplaces get so caught up in talking while selling that they forget to listen to the customer. Salespeople can see the person that walks by the store or into their area as a possible sale, not as a human being. If their manager is watching and the manager's priority is sales numbers, the salesperson really works on the customer as a project or challenge. You can hear the salesperson pull out all their sales techniques, like "overcoming the customer's objections" and "finding their hot buttons." Sadly, the salesperson is only applying techniques, and there is little service going on. It is as if the salesperson was trying to win a battle or achieve a goal but not connect with and affect the life of the customer in a positive way. To make a difference, the salesperson has to listen to the customer and genuinely want to help that person. The salesperson needs to take an interest in the customer, not as a means to an end but as an end in itself. If you observe our fishmongers, you will hear them asking things like, "Where are you from?" "What are you having for dinner?" "What's in your shopping bag?" All these questions come from the interest they take in the customer. Of course, the fishmongers' focused listening is far more important than the questions they ask.

If you are going to listen powerfully to your customers, you can't do it in order to make more money. If you do listen for that reason, it is just a form of manipulation. You are going to be listening through the filter of "Come on, say yes." Or, "Come on! You can spend more than that." When you truly listen to someone, you hold that person in high regard. You see him or her as naturally valuable with something significant to contribute.

In the early days of World Famous Pike Place Fish, we spent a lot of time exploring what it meant to take an interest in people. Jim helped us with exercises that showed the staff the distinction between connecting with distractions and connecting with a crewmember or customer. The exercises clearly illustrated the effects of being distracted by thoughts or other activities and the way these distractions result in very divided attention. By contrast, participants were able to see how powerfully they could connect with another person when they committed to listening to make a difference. We seldom do these exercises with the staff nowadays because they are expert listeners. We do, however, routinely provide this training opportunity to business clients and those who attend the Flying Fish/bizFutures World Famous 101 courses.

Our staff has truly incorporated "listening to make a differ-

ence" into their way of being with one another and with customers. They offer one another and the people they serve a safe
environment to have the experience of being known and appreciated. For example, a couple of my guys were talking to two customers in wheelchairs. As they took an interest in the customers,
they found out that the men were from New York and that they
were on vacation in Seattle. One of these customers shared that
as they had planned their trip they looked forward to "coming to
Pike Place Fish." At one point in the conversation, the customers
started showing the crewmembers all the features of their electric
wheelchairs. In fact, one of my guys noted that it was "like a
rocket ship." Before you knew it, the crew had navigated the customers behind the counter. Their wheelchairs allowed them to be
raised up high enough to actually catch fish thrown at them from
the front of the stand, and the customers were elated.

Those two men from New York bought T-shirts to com-
memorate their visit and later wrote the fishmongers a thank-you
letter. In it they expressed how "their experience at Pike Place
Fish exceeded anything they could have hoped for." It was
through my team member's listening to make a difference that
he became aware of the importance of Pike Place Fish to these
two customers' vacation. This way of listening also opened up an
understanding of how our crew could serve them in a world
famous way.

CREATING A LISTENING ZONE AROUND YOUR WORKPLACE

It is sad how many people are walking around with a deep need and desire to be heard. This large, unfilled need makes being with people all the more important and rewarding. Service to customers at Pike Place Fish really is about listening in such a way that we take all of the attention off ourselves and place it on the customers. We're out to discover how to make their lives better. We're out to have our customers leave our shop with the *experience* that they have been served. We want them to feel known and appreciated whether or not they buy fish. And it's not good enough just to want that—it takes an unrelenting commitment. We've made it our job to make sure that the experience of being served happens for every customer and in each interaction of the team members. To that end, we work with the crew to create a great environment for people so that they can be heard from a hundred feet away. Our staff learns to find the opportunity to listen to people even before they get to the fish stand. As people emerge from a distance, our staff begins to look for an opportunity to listen for their needs.

The benefits of powerful listening are demonstrated by the kind comments we get from our customers. Whether it is the way we handle complaints or the way we fill orders, we keep listening, and people keep sharing. Customers acknowledge the difference my staff members make in a variety of ways. We are sent acknowledgments that include tips, presents, e-mail messages, cards, and letters. A steady stream of caps, T-shirts, and even home-baked goods are offered as thanks for our team's incredible customer service. We also receive great messages on our website, such as, "Some of my teammates took me out to your market when we were in Seattle on business. It was a lot of fun, and it was great to . . . watch you guys in action, and buy a lot of T-shirts that I probably won't be able to expense, but was glad I could get one for everyone anyway! I also got some great pictures that I will send as soon as I am back in the office . . . You guys probably get about a million of these e-mails a day, but I wanted to let you know that you have a lot of admirers out there who really look up to you . . . Keep up the great attitude, you are doing wonderful things for people. Thank You!!!—Laura."

HANDLING CUSTOMER COMPLAINTS

While it's fairly easy to listen intently when people are praising you, it can get more challenging when customers are screaming and unhappy. Because of that, we spend a lot of time training employees to take complaints in person and on the phone. For example, we examine what happens when people call and are upset about not getting everything they ordered in their shipment. No matter how bad the caller's attitude may be, we work to listen for the opportunity to make a difference for the person during that call without aggravating the situation. Our effectiveness results from being really calm, coming from a positive intention, and being interested in what the customer has to say. The key to our success in listening is that we allow the person to communicate without being interrupted. Often it is about just listening and allowing the caller to vent his or her entire upset. It's about being open no matter what the customer has to communicate. It is in allowing the person the room to safely express his or her feelings that we find out what we can do, in light of the error, to make a difference. Our people have the power to do whatever it takes to make a difference for the customer. They can make any customer service decision they choose (replace an item, offer them free product—whatever is needed to serve the customer). As long as my staff is listening to make a difference and acting from that intention, they have the authority as co-owners of the vision to do what it takes for the customer.

I wonder whether someone has truly listened to you lately. Do you typically listen to make a difference, or do you usually listen to defend yourself? It is your choice!

|VII|

Coaching for Greatness

From Minnows to Whales

DEVELOPING A PEER-COACHING CULTURE

IMAGINE A WORKPLACE WHERE PEOPLE ARE constantly coaching one another. A place where employees welcome the opportunity to give feedback to and receive it from their coworkers and where their choices to coach come from a deep commitment to live the company's vision and to lift up coworkers to do the same. Some of you may be thinking it sounds like fantasyland—we call it Pike Place Fish.

While many owners and managers may think they want an environment where team members actively coach one another, they need to prepare themselves for the reality of open and honest communication. Many employers say they'd like an energetic, vocal, creative, and dynamic team, but when they actually experience people expressing constructive ideas, they are confronted with the prospect of being coached themselves. People who just want to be the "boss" don't want to hear the creative ideas of their employees. I know all about that management style from the days when I was the "boss" and I set the rules. When I committed to having a coaching culture in my company, I committed myself to being coachable. It turns out that to be a great coach you have to be wide open to receiving coaching from any-where—from everyone you meet—and particularly from your employees.

When our crewmembers make their commitment to World Famous Pike Place Fish, they are asked to take ownership of the vision. When that commitment happens, everyone owns the company and everyone associated with Pike Place Fish works to fulfill that vision for one another. Then, when someone sees a team member not being the vision, he is naturally called to step in and empower that person. Our team's ability to make a difference for customers is enhanced when each staff member offers his experience, creativity, and input to teammates so that all can perform at their highest level.

To make our team, people must be coachable. Many people are attracted to Pike Place Fish because they think it is a glamorous job and they can become a celebrity. The game really starts when a coworker asks a new hire to take out the garbage or when the new fishmonger has invested forty-five minutes setting up the crab display only to be told by a coworker, "You might think that you did it right, but in the next hour and a half when the ice melts, the crabs will fall on the ground, so you need to take it all down and set it up again." It is in those moments that new employees discover how coachable they are.

BECOMING COACHABLE

All of us have a certain amount of resistance to change and to fulfilling our commitments to others. We may claim that we will serve something larger than ourselves (a marriage, family, organization, workplace), but when it is time to stand for that commitment, our egos often get in the way. Rather than accepting coaching that serves the good of the team, we get caught up in wanting to do things our own way. Imagine the tension that occurs when twelve fishmongers challenge a new hire's ego by giving continual suggestions on making a world famous difference, selling fish, and being excellent. At times, it feels like you just can't do anything right—until you give up your ego and get with the program. Then that very same coaching can empower you.

Just about everybody who comes to work for us has to go through a process of becoming open to coaching. Not all of them realize it. We have people who have been on sports teams and think they know what teams are all about. They will say things like, "You are not coaching me the right way. I don't like the way you said that." Or, "I don't mind that you coach me, but I have to know why. Why should I do it this way?" Some of our new employees have had experiences at other fish markets. When our team members offer them coaching they say, "I already know this stuff." If they don't let go of that attitude, they are not going to make our team.

People become open to coaching at their own pace and in

their own way. In the early days, Jim and I invested a great deal of time and energy to move my team members to a place where they could give and receive coaching. We slowly but surely created a safe environment in our meetings, and we discussed the power that comes from being open to changing certain ideas and beliefs. At first we created some simple structures to help the crew understand how to coach effectively. We used exercises that showed how to identify and communicate needed changes while safely sharing feedback. Our team gained experience and insights with the challenges of both giving and receiving coaching. Once our staff gained this new understanding from the experiential training, we threw out that structure and encouraged them to openly coach one another.

Today the team helps new staff members both become coachable and initiate effective coaching. In fact, the team gives so much feedback to a new hire that it becomes fairly obvious that they see the individual's potential and greatness. Their coaching demonstrates their commitment to their new team member. In the beginning, new hires often don't understand that they are being coached for their own benefit and can find themselves caught up in disempowering ideas, such as, "Everybody is against me here!" Or, "People are always on my case." Once new hires appreciate that coaching comes from the commitment others have for their success, they experience the true bonding and synergy of being on our team.

People can truly feel when a team is in sync. I can see it with our staff when I walk by the market. When customers place an order with a fishmonger up front and he calls it back to the crew behind the counter, all our staff responds to the order by repeating it in unison. The timing and force of that call and response are a gauge of our team's unity. I know if the guys are in one voice when they repeat, "One king salmon." When the team is unified in their rhythm not only do I know, but more important, the crowd knows. People are drawn to that level of cohesion. There is something magical about teamwork and the beauty of people operating flawlessly as one. When our team is really in a groove, you could stop the action and ask them what they're experiencing, only to find that they have lost themselves inside the group. Their reality is completely the reality of the group and the group's common intention. Coaching is a vehicle that allows people to stay aligned with one another. It is the glue that binds the team together.

CONVERSATIONS THAT LIMIT THE STAFF'S WILLINGNESS TO COACH

When I ask people what is more difficult, giving or receiving coaching, most tell me that offering feedback is more challenging. While the key to receiving coaching involves staying open and avoiding defensiveness, the difficulties associated with giving coaching range from not wanting to cause trouble, to not caring enough about a coworker to make a difference, to concluding in advance that the person won't accept the coaching or use it to improve. At Pike Place Fish, we view all of these limiting factors as internal conversations. If my staff were to continue to identify themselves with these conversations, then no coaching could ever occur. Let's look at some conversations that interfere with offering coaching and examine how Jim and I have worked with our team to see other ways to view them.

"It's Easier to Do It Myself."

The other day, one of my fishmongers saw a few clams misaligned and not rotated correctly on our display. He walked up to the clam bench and started to rearrange them. It would have taken him ten seconds to adjust them in the appropriate way. As he reached out to fix the clams, he realized that he was working from a conversation that goes, "This will be easier for me to fix than it will be to coach the person who set this up incorrectly." Once he caught himself in that conversation, he chose a different one: "I owe it to the person who did this to offer my experience so that he can do it right the next time." He then went out of his way to identify who set up the clam display. He took the time to offer coaching about what he saw that needed fixing, and the feedback was well received. In the long run, that employee actually saved time, particularly if, over and over again, he continued to fix the problem instead of helping his teammate figure out how to do it right in the first place. More important, the team member acted on his belief that his coworker was a highly skilled, professional fishmonger who sets up great displays. While this may seem to be a small example, it is the small things, if not addressed, that frequently turn into the large things. It is also out of a willingness to live your commitment to others that you actually coach them to be their best in both large and small ways.

"Why Should I Coach Them?
They Are Not Going to Take It Well."

One of my guys pulled me aside and told me he was having a hard time coaching one of his teammates. He said that every time he starts to coach the other guy, he thinks that the person is going to be angry and retaliate. Because of an incident that never got resolved, he believes the other person will say, "We don't need you here." He noticed that he "walked on eggshells" around the other guy. As we talked, I coached him. I pointed out how his interpretation of the past encounter was shaping the way he dealt with his teammate. He realized that he might or might not be able to change the other person's willingness to listen to him, but he *could* change his own willingness to make a difference for his teammate. By doing so, he could invite his teammate to create a more powerful relationship. I offered him no sympathy but rather encouraged him to take responsibility for his situation. My commitment is to both of the employees and to the entire team. This fishmonger later shared that he had stopped identifying with the past incident. He said that after our conversation, he no longer felt intimidated and has created a new relationship with his teammate. He now gives him effective coaching.

"What's the Use?
I've Told Them This Before and It Hasn't Changed."

In a meeting, one of our managers shared how he overcame an internal conversation that limited his willingness to coach others. He noticed that he got upset with people after he had talked to them four or five times about what needed to be done. From his perspective, the issues he was raising simply required common sense. He essentially had given up on people who hadn't incorporated his coaching. He realized that by not offering coaching, he was choosing to be more committed to being right about his view of his teammates than he was to helping them create a better future. This need to be correct in his assessments made him an ineffective coach. When he committed to being an excellent coach, he stopped assessing people and instead inspired their greatness; he saw their uniqueness and helped them to be their best.

"They Have More Experience Than I Do. What Do I Have to Offer Them?"

One new employee found it hard to coach anyone on staff. His conversation went something like this: "Some of these guys have been here forever. What could I offer them?" He really believed that his lack of experience meant that he had nothing to share with his teammates. I was excited to show him a new reality. Like all situations where employees are working to find their personal power, it was important to point out the reasonableness of his interpretation, but I enjoyed supporting him in discovering that his beliefs were not necessarily true. His perspective certainly seemed true to him. I pointed out how he produced situations in his head and looked for data to confirm his ideas and beliefs. I invited him to change the conversation he was working from into something more productive, like, "I have a brand-new, unbiased view and have something to offer." By making that shift, he reported that he became aware that "People who have been doing things the same way for a long time can often slack on them and they can also miss new and creative ways to get things done."

When coaching is working well, it's because the coach is good at creating a culture of empowerment. Effective coaches are no longer judging others but instead are taking responsibility for what they themselves are doing. They are suggesting and recommending, not ordering. They are inviting people to check alternative ways of thinking and being. They actually encourage other people to take charge of themselves. Coaching reflects a person's deeply held commitment to empower teammates into action.

By contrast, coaching fails when a person isn't operating from an intention to assist others. Instead, the coach may be interested in proving that her teammates are wrong or may want to dominate her peers. I was guilty of that type of poor coaching when my brother took over as manager. Every time I saw Dicky do something that I didn't approve of, I was eager to make him wrong. I remember stopping by the market one day and discovering that we were running out of fish. Dicky told me that we had a shipment of fish waiting to be picked up at the airport. Upon hearing that, I went off, "How come you haven't picked that up already? Don't you have any sense of urgency about this stuff?" I wasn't sharing my upset to help Dicky grow into a better manager. I was firing on him as incompetent and worthless.

Often coaching breaks down when one person gets upset over something that another person did. Rather than discuss the problem, the person with the upset does nothing. Invariably, the

"The greatest good you can do for another is not to share your riches, but to reveal to him his own."

—BENJAMIN DISRAELI

offending party does the same behavior again, and again, the person who is upset takes no action. Finally, when the offender acts the same way yet again, the offended person retaliates in the name of coaching.

GETTING PAST YOUR EGO—OPENING UP TO COACHING

In the beginning, we at Pike Place Fish were just like anyone else when it came to having egos and anxieties surface as we were being coached. What ultimately made the difference was that we practiced a new way of relating to one another every day and that gave us many opportunities to master our resistance. Through constant coaching and Jim's ongoing support at meetings, we were continually made aware of our struggles to listen openly and to change. We learned that some of the conversations that get in the way of listening to each other include the following:

"I Don't Want to Change.
I Like Things the Way They Are."

You would think that all the staff members who transitioned through the harsh management days at the market would have welcomed the greater creative freedom and respect they were offered through the new empowering vision. However, a few of our veteran guys actually missed the way things used to be. One of them said, "Things are getting too loose around here. I liked it better when the boss made the rules and told me what to do. People are getting away with a lot more stuff now. Things used to run tighter around here."

It is impossible to be powerful in the present when your conversation is about "how things were back then." You can't create your future from "back then." You can only create it in the here and now. If you choose to indulge conversations about "back then," you will get stuck "back there." The people who stepped into our vision of World Famous Pike Place Fish repeatedly and consistently chose to shift to a conversation that placed them in the present. Actually, the most powerful creativity occurs when you suspend how things "were" and how things "should be" and start from a new beginning. It is much easier to create on a blank canvas than on one that already has a picture present.

"I Don't Like the Way You Are Coaching Me, So I Am Not Listening."

In an ideal world, all coaching at Pike Place Fish would go something like this:

> *"Dicky, can I coach you now?"*
> *"Sure, Johnny."*
> *"Dicky, you went to lunch without telling anybody. Can you let me know next time?"*
> *"Sure, Johnny. Thanks for coaching me."*

In an even better situation, Dicky would ask for coaching on an issue for which he felt a need for assistance.

Optimally, when I offer Dicky coaching, I would ask his permission. He would then have the opportunity to either accept the offer, counteroffer a better time, or turn the offer down altogether. If he chose not to hear the feedback at all, his world famous commitment would lead him to seek me out later to discuss what I had to say.

Once Dicky had given me permission to coach him, I'd offer coaching quickly without justification. I wouldn't try to convince him that there was a good reason for what I was saying. He would listen for my input knowing that I was giving him an opportunity to grow. He wouldn't argue the details of my coaching by saying something like, "I told another guy to tell you. It's his fault that you didn't know." Dicky would realize that he could take or leave my coaching. He would accept the part of what I had to say that benefited him and reject the rest. He would be able to see that my coaching was nothing more than my interpretation of the situation and not the ultimate truth. Dicky would acknowledge that he had heard me and that he could see the benefit of my sharing. Finally, he would let me know that he appreciated the coaching.

Based on the commitment I have made to my staff, I strive to coach as effectively as possible, but when fifty to a hundred customers are crowded around the fish stand on a summer day, coaching doesn't always turn out optimally. I might actually say to Dicky, "Where the heck have you been? I need to know when you leave the market." So what would Dicky do with that feedback? It is likely that he would have an ego reaction to my flawed coaching. Clearly, I started by making Dicky wrong. But would he choose to let his justification run him? If so, he would likely say, "To heck with you. Maybe you should check around before you start making allegations. I did let people know where I was going." If he made that choice, our conversation and relationship would go downhill from there. Or Dicky could simply say, "Okay." By doing so, he would accept the part of my coaching that was of value (that it would be helpful to me if he told me directly that he was going to lunch) and leave all of the "you were wrong" part of my coaching behind. When things were less hectic, Dicky could offer me some coaching about the way I coached him. This would be particularly of value if he had any remaining upset. Unless I made a habit of "making him wrong" during coaching, it is likely that Dicky could accept the useful part of my coaching and choose not to react to my upset. He could move past the entire incident.

"I Already Know How to Do It."

I am amused when a new employee's ego resists coaching because he already "knows how to do the job." Heck, I own the place. I've been at Pike Place Fish for thirty-five years, but when I go to work at the market, I get a lot of coaching. For example, I got coached about the way I call out orders. I would yell out a customer's order, "One Dungeness crab packaged for forty-eight hours going to Chicago." One of my guys said, "Come here, boss. Here's some coaching. Use five words, five words or less, like, 'Dungeness crab going to Chicago.' We can't repeat whole sentences." I said, "Okay, I got it—one crab, forty-eight-hour pack." My staff member's coaching quickly helped me realize that the packers can get the details at the counter. I understood that the busy crew wouldn't remember all the details and certainly wouldn't echo back a response when my call was a whole sentence.

No matter how much we think we know how to do things (I've been working at the market longer than most of my employees have been alive), the only way we can grow and create is to choose conversations that give us power.

"Before I Do What You Ask, Tell Me Why."

On a Saturday afternoon when the market is jam-packed, it's not unusual for a manager to ask a team member to go into the cooler and get a certain kind of fish. Occasionally, you will hear a fishmonger ask the manager why that fish is needed and why it is needed right then. Rather than acting on the request, the fishmonger doesn't want to move until the feedback makes sense to him. It would be like a quarterback in the huddle telling a wide receiver to run a certain pass route, only to have the receiver ask him why he wants that route run. Jim and I work with our crew so that they will stay open to the information they are receiving from one another. We help crewmembers see that there are appropriate times to seek understanding and that these times typically aren't in the middle of heated action. We emphasize the importance of taking peer coaching so that ultimately the team performs well.

IT'S NOT THOUGHTS, BUT CONVERSATIONS

Some people may conclude that Pike Place Fish's management approach is one of changing the thoughts of our employees so they are willing to coach and be coached more effectively. I am uncomfortable with the word "thoughts." It may seem subtle, but thoughts are made up of words, and the power of thoughts comes from the specific words we use. Our effort at the World Famous Pike Place Fish Market is to uncover power-limiting words—or conversations, if you will—so our crewmembers can choose more powerful alternatives. That is why we insist that our crewmembers stay open to coaching by shifting from conversations like "I already know how to do this" to conversations like "What can I gain from the coaching I received about how to do this?" It is also the reason we encourage fishmongers to stay more open to coaching by letting go of conversations like "It is easier to do it myself" and instead choose conversations such as "I am committed to teach my coworker how to do it correctly."

We are absolutely clear that our words and interpretations shape our reality. When my staff members examine the words that get in the way of their power and share their observations through coaching, they learn ways to change our workplace. If we don't bring these words and conversations to the surface, they will remain as thoughts locked inside a box and change will be unlikely. Great coaches help people recognize power-limiting conversations and move beyond them, concentrating instead on creating powerful ones. From my perspective, coaching is a lot like fishing—you keep the big fish and leave the smaller ones behind.

When it comes to coaching, Pike Place Fish is a strange place. It is odd to see a corporate culture where feedback is so readily given and so graciously received. Defensiveness and resistance to change have melted away, and people now see coaching as an opportunity for growth. At Pike Place Fish, things get done better than ever before, and our people are at their creative best. The success of our coaching starts with our staff's intention to make a world famous difference and our commitment to care enough to consistently share supportive, compassionate comments and ideas with one another. While unusual, our culture is available to any workplace. It's just a conversation away.

Turning Workplace Challenges into Breakthroughs

Unsnagging the Line

AVOIDING THE TRAP OF BLAME

IN THE OLD DAYS AT PIKE Place Fish, every time something went wrong, I was looking for someone to blame. When a shrimp fell on the floor, I wanted to know who had knocked it off and make sure that the person knew they'd screwed up. I thought that blame was what accountability was about. Nowadays, I know that problems, snags, breakdowns, and even crises serve as opportunities for us to grow in our ability to live our vision.

We experience many setbacks, frustrations, disappointments, and conflicts at Pike Place Fish. But like most evolving companies, we see fewer and fewer of these problems all the time. We can't ignore, however, that over the years, Pike Place Fish has had its share of disputes between crewmembers, major team power struggles, missed business objectives, temporary supply problems, and intermittent lapses in our commitment to be our vision.

The fishmongers and I now know that when problems occur, we can choose our reactions. Instead of looking for blame and getting stuck in figuring out what went wrong, each of us chooses to let our commitment to make a difference for people guide us. Our team sees each problem as an opportunity to create a new arena in which to play. Without our vision, I am sure we would go back to being run by our righteousness, and ultimately, our business would be a disaster.

These days, I view each workplace challenge as an opportunity to break through to a new level of making a difference. As we work through problems, we deepen our understanding of our vision and strengthen our commitment to one another. At Pike Place Fish, our breakdowns offer us a chance to create more of a difference. It isn't that we are perfect and instantly see every problem as an opportunity. We *are* human beings. The difference between us and other companies, however, is that we have made a commitment to choose our vision and not get caught up in our personal point of view.

Not unlike most small and large businesses, we find the bulk of our snags at Pike Place Fish occur in upsets among staff members. Usually these problems take the form of one-on-one conflicts, but occasionally they turn into actual team breakdowns.

Snag 1—One-on-One Communication

When we first made our commitment to be world famous, we created an environment where it was safe for people to commu-

"Help your brother's boat across, and you will reach the shore."

—HINDU PROVERB

nicate their upsets. We used our staff meetings to train the whole team, and we made sure to support people as they took responsibility for their own experiences. Every time a conflict between two people was processed at a meeting, every team member who was present could benefit from the dispute resolution process. Now, team members handle most disagreements right as they occur; they seldom store their upsets for a meeting a week or two later. By addressing issues on the spot, they not only clear up conflicts more quickly, but also allow our staff meetings to focus on the future instead of the past.

Most of the problems I've seen occur between people are in the area of communication. Given our emphasis on open listening and active coaching, all of us at Pike Place Fish take responsibility for our interpretation of events that occur on the job. As such, our fishmongers have gotten very good at handling most communication problems by themselves. If a conflict is getting in the way of a member's ability to empower the team, he asks the person he is having a problem with to step into the office or the cooler and talk things over. This beats the heck out of the days when conflicts actually came to blows. Today, when crewmembers get upset with each other, they take a moment and handle it. When teammates don't resolve disputes, the manager takes them aside and offers coaching on how to move beyond their conflict. In addition to resolving conflicts, we have committed to using disputes to create a new, deeper relationship among team members.

Our people play games with one another. They tease one another and poke and jab in a way our staff calls "swordplay." Most of it is in good fun and is carried out in a spirit of playfulness. This playfulness is something our crewmembers share not only with one another but with our customers as well. Sometimes, however, the swordplay goes too far. One morning, a senior employee came up to me and confessed that he had tapped a junior employee in the groin with a wrench while the junior employee was on a ladder. The less experienced worker was in the office with one of the managers saying that he was upset and wanted to go home. I went into the office and invited the young man to have a conversation with me to see whether we could resolve his upset. Through our conversation, we discovered together that even though he said he had forgiven his teammate, he had not. Once he realized he was hooked by his anger and feelings of victimization, he was able to choose to genuinely forgive. More significant, he stayed on the job that day and used the situation to improve the relationship with his senior colleague. The older employee realized that he had blamed the younger one for being too sensitive and had not taken responsibility for his own actions. Once he understood that he was blaming his teammate, he acknowledged that he was the one who had hurt his younger crewmember.

Some of you are probably thinking, "Wait! Sometimes people really are victims of others." My reply is, "What you say is what you get." If you tell yourself that is the case, then that is the case. It will likely become your reality. At Pike Place Fish, we have committed to leaving people empowered, not victimized.

Over the years, we have had some employees with overpowering and aggressive personalities. One staff member was an ex-convict. When he was first hired, he was a street fighter with very little mercy for his fellow crewmembers. It was almost as if he had radar for the weakest member of the team. He would focus his most vicious attacks on his identified victim. This guy would belittle his target. He would look for every mistake the man made and then call him on those mistakes. Worse yet, he would try to enlist other people in his verbal attacks. For a while, his favorite victim was a crewmember who had a history of being beaten by his father. Anytime anyone raised his or her voice at work, this vulnerable guy would literally disappear. This preferred "victim" was always very apologetic. Because we are committed to making a difference for people, everybody gets coached. In this situation, we attempted to enable the "bully" and the "victim" to give up their habits and make a difference for each other and the team. Both individuals grasped that they had to take responsibility for their own experiences and that no one was doing anything to anyone. They each created their reality.

Snag 2—From Individual Problems to Team Distress

On rare occasions our people do not address their upsets directly but instead gossip to other teammates, hoping to enlist them on their side. I had a staff member who reminded me of myself at a younger age. This guy was intense and passionate about excellence. Unfortunately, he had no clue about what it took to coach others. Whenever he saw someone doing something he considered "wrong," he'd yell at them. As you might expect, this behavior frequently angered his teammates. As the anger toward him rose, several of his peers wanted him fired. In fact, at one of our meetings, one fishmonger stated, "Either he leaves or I leave." Having heard this, our would-be coach gained a deep insight into how he had alienated his crewmembers. When he understood their feelings toward him, he said, "I have something I want to say. I apologize." He then went around the table and said to each person, "I want you to get that I love you. Do you understand that?" He went on to promise that he would change and asked to remain on the team. With that, the individuals who had been against him changed their perception of him and understood that he was actually committed to their excellence. They then decided to help him be a great coach.

Snag 3—Losing Focus on the Vision

At Pike Place Fish our breakdowns aren't always individual communication difficulties or team conflicts; sometimes we simply get pulled into a way of being that is not consistent with our vision. One of the most upsetting times for me was when we had business guests in town. Managers from as far away as Singapore had come to the market to learn about our business success. While in Seattle these guests spent time with Jim, the fishmongers, and me. The fishmongers have at least three important contributions they make for interested business leaders: (1) they share their own experiences and insights on empowerment and culture; (2) they answer the manager's questions about teamwork, living the vision, and choosing effective conversations; and (3) they coach the guests as they help the crew set up the fish show during one of the mornings of their stay. On one such morning, I came down to watch the interaction between the business leaders and our fishmongers. There were several of our team members helping the guests set up the shows and three other crewmembers in the back of the shop. To my shock and horror, the three guys behind the counter had their backs turned to our guests and were laughing, working, and talking among themselves. I was mad and pulled these three employees aside, asking them to look at "who they were being." I shared that in the past, "I would have fired you on the spot for that kind of behavior." I asked each of them, "Is this what you are committed to being?" I went on to tell them, "The conversation that is running you right now is, 'forget these people.' They came here to actually experience you empowering one another. This is crap." That's all I said. They all got it and turned around. Each of them said, "I'm sorry." Then I left. I came back five minutes later, and they were making a difference for the visiting managers. It is amazing, but three veteran team members got hooked into their own little world and forgot what they were there to do. All of us fall asleep on our commitment at times. The key is being coachable so that you can instantly choose to get back to your commitment when you get input from others.

Snag 4—Failing to Meet Business Objectives

For all businesses, large and small, it is important to manage problems that affect the bottom line and profitability. At times, the Pike Place Fish Market experiences setbacks in meeting our monthly sales objectives or some other business target. We project our sales goals monthly. We look at performance in past years and declare a goal for sales that month. Our staff attempts to break our own records month-to-month and across similar quarters of the year.

December is an incredible month for us, and we can reliably

expect a large drop in sales for January. Nonetheless, we set an ambitious but attainable goal given prior January sales numbers. When a recent January ended and we had missed our projected sales by a fairly significant number, I opened our next staff meeting by asking people to explore what had gotten in the way of our goal. I personally owned up to my willingness to buy into the conversation "It is January and it's always slow." My staff then shared a set of conversations in which they had indulged that ultimately interfered with their making the projected sales goal. One team member noted, "When I saw that we were far away from our prediction by the twentieth of the month, I just slacked off. I stopped generating sales as I had been earlier." Another indicated that he had convinced himself "that money was tight for people in January and that most people had overspent at Christmas, the same as me." Yet another acknowledged that with fewer customers at the market, he felt he was "intruding on those that came by." Given this perception, he acknowledged that he was more reluctant to engage passersby in conversation. Yet another fishmonger concluded that a downturn in the economy was limiting sales. By understanding how each of us yielded our personal power ("We're not going to make goal." "They overspent like me." "I'm intruding." "It's the fault of a bad economy."), we could choose different conversations to help us generate more sales in the future.

Insight offered us a chance to break through our self-imposed sales limits. Simply by being honest about the things that each of us bought into, we could challenge our assumptions. In turn, this challenge could help us generate new possibilities and a more profitable future. For example, I asked, "Was it our intention to intrude or was it our intention to make a difference? Did everyone overspend at Christmas? Is everyone like us?" These questions were offered to help the team realize that they were making up their own reality. Once people see that they are creating conversations of failure, they are in a place to generate a more powerful outcome. Will the staff choose to create scarcity or generate abundance? By missing our goal that January, we were given the opportunity to commit anew. Those January sales difficulties and our reactions to them provided Pike Place Fish the chance to generate an even more profitable future. The day after that meeting we had the single largest purchase in our history.

Snag 5—Sales but No Profit

Sometimes workplace problems sneak up on you. For example, we had a record-breaking August. We exceeded all sales projections and, for the first time, even eclipsed prior December sales. It was absolutely unbelievable. What was more surprising was that there was no profit sharing that month. In fact, we actually lost money that August. Record sales and no profit, how could that be? What a great opportunity for our team!

That August gave us the chance to distinguish between sales and profitability. We had been so busy selling that we hadn't appreciated how much product we were wasting and how sloppy we had been with inventory. While this is not necessarily the way someone wants to learn a lesson, waste showed up to help us understand that sales were not enough. Over a series of meetings, the crew explored breakdowns in profitability. These missteps included not rotating stock, faulty ordering decisions, and letting our crab thaw out. Our lack of profitability that month taught me, as an owner, that our crew needed a better understanding of costs and expenses. We began exploring profitability as a way of being. Jim and I wanted our staff to get a smell for profitability so they could know when it was and was not happening. As a team, we created a profitability distinction and started breaking records in both sales and profit—amazing records! The team kept their sales volume high and decreased the waste. We didn't want sales volume to decrease in the name of profitability, as sales are always important in a seasonal business. We wanted the crew to gain awareness and take responsibility not only for sales but also for the bottom line. This distinction has paid off, as we now consistently break our monthly profitability records.

Snag 6—Decisions That Misalign with Commitments

Not long ago, I gained a major insight about our slow season. It was a personal breakthrough. After seeing great sales in December, I used to become depressed about sales in the slow months of January and February. Every year I faced the same emotional challenge. Should I lay people off or just lose money in January and February? In the old days, it was routine to let people go during the slow season. Fishmongers as a rule understand the seasonal nature of the work, and many of them hire on a month at a time on fishing boats. They are paid well for working on the boats and typically don't seem to mind being off when sales are slower at the market. Jim and I had many conversations about the pros and cons of layoffs during our slow season. The biggest benefit from layoffs was a decrease in my guaranteed losses in our slowest months. The largest risk from layoffs was that veteran crewmembers might not be available when the busier season returned. As such, I would be left with a less-seasoned workforce in busier times.

A business case could be made for either course of action— layoffs or staff retention. The breakthrough for me came by reexamining my intentions and letting the World Famous Pike Place Fish vision guide me. If I was truly committed to making my employees' lives great, I needed to offer them year-round employment even through lean months. Once I realized this, I no longer had a decision to make each January and February. I had broken through and taken a stand to care for my people. I accepted my financial losses. I was no longer depressed about the numbers in January and February. I saw those losses as part of my contribution to making a world famous difference for my crew.

Snag 7—Inventory Breakdowns

Black Mouth salmon weren't selling. We were losing money on them. My staff told me, "People don't like the Black Mouth. They just didn't want those 'number twos.' Can't you find us any Troll King salmon?" Managers get paid to solve problems. So I was tempted to reexamine all my options for finding Troll Kings, knowing full well that there were none to be had. Instead, I decided to work with our crew to create a breakthrough on the sale of Black Mouth salmon. As I explored our team's views about the Black Mouth, it became clear that people weren't buying that fish because our team had little passion for selling "number twos." They had somehow convinced themselves that Black Mouth salmon lacked quality when compared to Troll Kings. The way the crew talked and thought about the Black Mouth affected the energy they brought to selling it. So it was time for me to stand up as a leader and create a new interpretation of the Black Mouth.

I told my team that Black Mouth salmon were misunderstood in our shop. Black Mouths are an incidental catch, meaning that they are caught along with other fish in gill nets, not with hook and line. Because these fish are caught in nets, some of the scales are knocked off and their bones can at times be seen poking through their meat. I realized that I needed to enroll my team in a new reality about Black Mouth salmon. I told them that none of the Black Mouths' limitations in appearance affected the quality of their flavor, particularly if they were sold while they were fresh. To truly empower the staff to shift their reality from Black Mouths as "number twos" to "Black Mouths as great eating-quality fish," I took a stand for the team to have a breakthrough with Black Mouth. I had crewmembers take the fish home and eat it. I even told them how to cook it.

The next day the guys came back raving about what a great-tasting fish the Black Mouth was. They realized that the problem with the Black Mouth had all along just been their conversations. The Black Mouth literally started flying off the counter. After that I had the odd challenge of finding enough Black Mouth to supply the sales demand that the crew created.

Snag 8—Denying People Opportunities to Share in Decision Making

Problems can occur on teams when leaders make decisions without asking for input from their staff. From the onset of our desire to make a difference, Jim and I wanted the financial success of Pike Place Fish to be directly shared with the fishmongers. Despite this desire, a breakdown occurred in making that goal a reality.

Opportunities arose for the fishmongers to travel to speaking engagements and share a portion of the speaking fees with both Jim and me. A snag happened concerning the distribution of the fishmongers' share. Originally, I had determined a formula for distributing profit. My decision came from a desire to reward employee loyalty based on their years of service to Pike Place Fish. When I became aware that some of my employees were dissatisfied with "my" reimbursement system, I was tempted to say, "If you are not grateful for my efforts to share profits from the speaking, we don't need to do it at all." I was able to let go of that conversation and see the complaining as an opportunity to create unity for the team. I requested that the fishmongers work together and create a system that felt comfortable to them. I simply asked that their solution honor my original intention of rewarding seniority.

The greatest objection to my plan was coming from three of the newest members of the team. They were not buying in to the plan that I'd proposed. If I had demanded their acceptance of my proposal and said, "Tough, take it or leave it," it is likely they would have been upset with the program. But by encouraging the team to generate new options within my guidelines, those who had objected discussed it with their team members and decided that my original proposal was fair and workable. At the next crew meeting the entire team reported that they were very comfortable with my distribution proposal and appreciated the opportunity to try to create viable alternatives even though they hadn't come up with any. The crew, Jim, and I now travel all over the world speaking to audiences and generating great profits in a way that satisfies us all.

By viewing problems as breakdowns and challenges, all of us at Pike Place Fish operate from the knowledge that awareness, creativity, and commitment produce breakthroughs. In our culture, these workplace difficulties are normalized and even welcomed as opportunities to move the business and the vision to the next level.

Snag 9—Too Much Success

Not all opportunities for growth emerge from workplace problems. In fact, sometimes overwhelming success serves as the great opportunity for a breakthrough, particularly because accomplishment can breed complacency. If you win the championship in the game you're playing, it is easy to stop generating success. When we start believing what is written about us and what people say about us, especially when customers treat us like celebrities, we are at great risk of losing our humility and failing to live our vision. When we think we have arrived at World Famous Pike Place Fish as if it were a destination rather than a way of being, we stop creating our future. Success is an opportunity for us to change our conversation from self-congratulation (the big ego trip) to one that keeps us on track with our commitment to make a difference.

For a long time, my goal was to retire in my early sixties with a winter home in Palm Springs, California, and my current home in Seattle for the remainder of the year. I certainly have achieved the financial success necessary to retire. Since I committed to a new vision, however, I have become aware of the sizable opportunities I have to make a difference in the world. I didn't even know that I would want to act on those opportunities. Financial success is no longer my sole purpose for being on this planet. I have actually discovered that making a difference for other human beings is something that fulfills my life's purpose. In times of success, breakthroughs not only are about creating more success but can be opportunities for us to make our lives matter. When people discover what it means to make a difference, it creates for them a new world and gives meaning to their work.

| I X |

Taking a Stand

Finding Your Fish Worth Catching

WALKING THROUGH THE PROCESS
FOR CHANGING YOUR WORKPLACE

I KNOW THE POWER OF THE principles I've shared in this book. I have seen our incredible transformation over fifteen years of success and positive impact! Coming from our simple intention to make a world famous difference, we've demonstrated what is possible when employees are truly empowered. We've shown what happens when you create a mighty purpose for your organization. We've proven that people can intentionally create their future and do it in a way that makes a difference for everyone. While I have dedicated individual chapters to these principles, I would like to piece them all together so you can envision the entire process and create your own game worth playing.

People and organizations know something unusual is going on at Pike Place Fish; when you are around our crew you can literally feel the energy and creativity of our workforce. The conversation we started about being world famous in a way that makes a difference for people has traveled the globe through videos and books. It comes back to us through the loyalty and kindness of those who walk by the market, visit our website, or attend our training sessions. The uniqueness of our culture has drawn an increasing number of companies to Seattle to explore the principles of our success and has required us to travel worldwide to create a space for breakthroughs to happen in varied industries.

By now I hope that I have inspired you in the limitless possibilities these principles can offer you in your work life and beyond. But knowing something is possible and doing something about that possibility are two very different things. The skeptical part of our brain frequently kicks into gear when we start thinking about change. We ask questions like, "How do I know this stuff will work for me?" "How will I get my people to buy in to create a powerful vision?" Or, "Will this be like every other new program we have tried? Will it be hot for a while but then fade away?" It's very natural to have these doubts show up in the beginning of your adventure. We all have a need to know the exact "how-tos," and certainly we've experienced the frustration of short-lived change. Even though these conversations are normal, they don't need to stop you. You can do something bold and audacious and leap headfirst into action simply by committing to your vision. Anyone can be a visionary and be the person who inspires others to make a difference. The groups of people you gather together can be in the workplace, in your family, and in your community. These principles are equally effective in each setting.

BRINGING OUR MARKET'S SUCCESS TO YOUR BUSINESS

Let's review the key steps in the transformation that took place at the World Famous Pike Place Fish Market. These steps will be presented in a sequence. Please note, however, that even though the process will definitely improve your culture, you will not always know how the changes will show up. This process is not static; the dynamic forces in our culture mean that we are constantly assessing and reworking what our vision looks like. Similarly, we are constantly challenging our negative conversations and enhancing our ability to listen to make a difference. The process never ends. The game is simply played at a higher level with time.

While it is difficult to separate out the key components behind any company's success, the following elements are at the foundation of ours:

1. Creating a vision of power and possibility as a team;

2. Enrolling and formalizing individual commitment and team alignment to the vision;

3. Helping team members distinguish between the state of being and the state of doing;

"You are not here merely to make a living. You are here to enable the world to live more amply, with greater vision, and with a finer spirit of hope and achievement. You are here to enrich the world. You impoverish yourself if you forget this errand."

—WOODROW WILSON

4. Having the leadership redefine themselves as effective agents of change;

5. Assisting team members in letting go of internal and external conversations that rob them of their personal power;

6. Guiding team members to listen to make a difference instead of listening to defend or blame;

7. Helping the crew live their commitment to one another through effective coaching; and

8. Assisting crew members as they turn snags into breakthroughs.

YOUR INVITATION

Outside of Pike Place Fish, the story of the fishmongers and the lessons of our success are presented to companies that send leaders and frontline workers to Seattle to participate in the Flying Fish/bizFutures course, World Famous 101: Creativity, Empowerment, and Making a Difference. Jim, the fishmongers, and I offer a rich, expanded set of experiences and lessons consistent with those highlighted in this book. Individuals and businesses that have participated in this training have achieved many successes. We have enjoyed helping businesses like Cattlemen's Steakhouse, Kitchen Kettle Village, and Shell Oil Company improve their customer service ratings, win prestigious awards, gain media attention, enhance workplace safety, develop team cohesion, and increase their morale, workplace fun, and overall profitability.

I encourage you to take these steps and use them to energize your workplace and your life in ways you see fit. I further invite you to create your own game worth playing and do the follow-up necessary to have it come alive in your home and workplace.

To those ends, let's take an example of a fictitious supermarket that has accepted my invitation and incorporated the insights I've shared throughout this book.

TEAM VISIONING

Imagine for a moment that a manager at a grocery store wants to create a more energized team. She is tired of the infighting among staff members and a culture of gossip, absenteeism, and turnover. As the manager, she has had her fill of staff members going through the motions of serving customers with little passion or energy for their jobs. She realizes that her team needs to align around a more powerful purpose. She sets aside times for the entire team to create a game worth playing. During these meetings, the manager establishes an environment where people can share all ideas and explore all possibilities about the greater meaning of their work. She does this simply by asking people to agree to listen with respect and without interruption to everyone's point of view. She asks her team members to examine the opportunity that their job offers them when it comes to having a positive impact on the world. Respecting the fact that the business must remain financially viable, she helps the team define a common purpose beyond "ordering, stocking, and selling" and "bottom-line profits." She knows that her people need a bigger game. They need a greater sense of purpose and satisfaction from their efforts. They need a compelling vision. This process of team exploration allows her staff to find the greatest purpose possible while still generating profits.

Like many people who attempt to create an environment in which others can define a greater purpose, this supermarket manager is challenged to establish a safe place for her staff to share openly and honestly. Many members of her team have learned how to say what they think other people want to hear but not necessarily what they passionately feel. They have been told that their thoughts and feelings are silly, misguided, or impossible. As the manager, she needs to draw out the honest thoughts and feelings of these employees. During the meetings, the store manager opens up possibilities instead of shooting down ideas.

The manager continually helps the team generate their vision from a clean slate. She works around people's tendency to be limited by what has been or what is likely to be. She reminds her team that their vision is a creation—it's their chance to color outside the lines of their experience and to declare a purpose worth living and working for.

I remember these challenges well. Our declared visions of world fame and then world peace certainly didn't emerge from a look back at our past. We had no track record that would have suggested that these were the obvious next steps in our journey. In fact, the notion of world fame seemed preposterous to me at the time. While both of these declarations (world fame and world peace) appeared daunting in the beginning, the only way they can ever occur is if someone envisions and creates them in each moment. It is through these types of powerful visions that the United States achieved manned spaceflight and Gandhi facilitated the liberation of India from British rule without needing to resort to violence. Someone once said that it was sad that Walt Disney never lived to see Disney World, only to be reminded that if Walt had never seen it, no one else would have either.

COMMITTING—INDIVIDUAL AND TEAM

Let's assume that the supermarket manager's team defined their game worth playing. They declared that their more meaningful purpose went beyond generating revenue and included "improving the quality of life for all they served." Much in the way we integrate our vision with our name, World Famous Pike Place Fish, the store manager and team summarized their vision into a short statement, "Improving Customers' Lives with Every Contact." This statement, although brief (fewer than eight words), communicated the essence of the vision. Once the store manager's team could clearly see the vision and make it real, they could act on it. In defining the vision, the team included short-term goals and clarified for themselves what this game made possible for them, for others, and for the world.

With the vision initially defined, the store manager invited her team members to individually declare their commitment to "improve the quality of life for those they served." In essence, each team member was given the opportunity to publicly tell their teammates, "By standing here in front of you and making this declaration, I commit myself to our vision of improving the quality of life for those with whom we come in contact." As each individual made this declaration, the other team members were empowered to hold that person accountable to live the vision. The supermarket manager then offered her commitment not only to the vision but also to support every other member of the team as they lived the vision. She encouraged all team members to expand their commitment beyond the vision and provide support to their teammates. In turn, each member of her staff verbally shared the commitment to lift up and support all members of the team as each person creates the vision themselves.

BEING VERSUS DOING

Once her staff had made these commitments, the supermarket manager helped them understand the difference between "being" and "doing." She shared the true nature of vision: that living a vision is not a function of planning and strategy but a matter of defining one's intention and responding to the world from that intention. She noted, "If you engage your work life as a person who improves the quality of customers' lives, that is who you are—it is your state of being. When that intention fails to guide you, you are being someone else." She emphasized to her staff the importance of checking in on themselves with a regular inquiry about who they were being. Similarly, she let her staff know how they could help one another by assisting other teammates in looking at who they were being (in relation to the vision) in a given situation. The store manager helped her team members understand that the things that show up in their lives often reflect who they were being. If world-class results were showing up for their customers and coworkers, they were likely being their commitment. When people fail to live their commitment, they are often confronted with less than desirable outcomes.

LEADERS CHANGING THEMSELVES

The store manager realized that effective change started with her. She knew that "the fish stinks from the head" and that she needed to explore those conversations in which she lost herself, that took her away from being the vision. She sought coaching and support as she shifted her way of being with staff. She explored her commitment to the greatness of each of her team members and dedicated herself to the success of her team.

EMPOWERING CONVERSATIONS

By sharing her experiences, the supermarket manager offered her staff insights into struggles she experienced choosing conversations that gave her greater power. She helped her team access their internal conversations that took them away from living the vision. Her team came to her for ideas on how to let go of power-limiting conversations. For example, she helped one team member see how his conversations about "staff shortages" and "inventory problems" reduced his power to improve the quality of life for those he served. Once he understood how power-limiting conversations were trapping him, he chose different conversations, realizing that no matter how many staff were present or how much product was in the store, he was always able to improve the lives of the people he encountered.

LISTENING

The store manager spent a considerable amount of time creating safe listening environments. She lived her own commitment to the vision by consistently being a person who encouraged staff members to move beyond their egos and defenses. The manager took a genuine interest in her coworkers and listened to them with an ear for making a difference in their lives both at work and beyond. She noticed that when people felt safe and loved, they did not hide their shortcomings or blame others for them; rather they talked openly about the choices they made that took them away from being the vision. Additionally, in a safe environment, people sought guidance for making more "on-vision" choices. They were willing to take feedback and use it to grow.

COACHING

The store manager helped her team appreciate that it is difficult both to give and to receive coaching from coworkers. She addressed the types of internal conversations that get in the way of effective coaching. While acknowledging these challenges, she re-emphasized the importance of living the commitment to help coworkers be their best. She dealt with increased conflict levels as team members grew in their ability to communicate and receive coaching constructively. She noticed that this conflict did not last long, as her staff quickly used the information they got from one another in constructive ways. Her staff coached one another readily, and she herself was getting regular feedback and coaching from everyone on her team.

SNAGS TO BREAKTHROUGHS

The supermarket manager derived a great sense of satisfaction from helping team members see that everyone has opportunities to evolve and grow and that problems serve as openings for growth to occur in the direction of the vision. She let go of her own resistance when offered feedback by others or when she became frustrated by a problem at work. She invited and welcomed feedback from everyone in the workplace and used this feedback to create breakthroughs at the store.

SUCCESS IS AN ONGOING PROCESS

I would love to tell you that the store manager lived happily ever after and that she never had to address any of these issues again, but that is not reality. In fact, it is likely that she would be further called upon as a source of power and energy for her staff's growth on a moment-by-moment basis. Her function, like that of all great leaders, would likely change with time. As her team matures, they would take on more and more of their own cultural development. She would no longer walk through a workplace where people are "just going through the motions." Instead, she would help the team channel all of their creative energy and ideas associated with improving the quality of life for customers.

I can feel a company's culture when I walk into a business. When people are working together for an important function, it shows. It is electric. It is even more apparent when each individual lets go of his own defenses to receive coaching from his teammates and when they offer feedback openly. For us, the creation of that culture required great commitment and constant support. People need assistance to understand the importance of listening to make a difference. They gain from support as they struggle against their defensiveness. My crew benefit from help in selecting more powerful conversations. With consistent and genuine interest in their growth, teams create amazing results.

SUCCESS STORIES BEYOND PIKE PLACE FISH

Many companies have come to Jim and me and defined their game worth playing. We have seen breakthroughs happen in industries as far ranging as retail, finance, and health care. Even groups and individuals have demonstrated the transforming power of commitment to a meaningful purpose. A school district in the Midwest committed to "wipe out illiteracy." They took a stand saying that every child would learn to read. Their game worth playing went beyond their own special education courses or reading classes. By committing to their powerful vision, they began exploring possibilities so that "every child from birth to ten years of age will be read to five times a week." Talk about a bold vision. They declared it—and it is now their way of being.

A paper company from the East Coast simply committed to "bridge gaps" no matter where they occurred. Their vision involved seeing needs in their workplace and world and being resources to fill those gaps. At World Famous Pike Place Fish, we talk about finding opportunities to make a difference; at this paper company they talk about seeing gaps that need to be bridged. In fact, the paper company displays images and replicas of bridges in their workplace to serve as quick reminders of their vision. No longer is their job simply about paper products; now their game is to bridge gaps in communication, relationships, teamwork, and accountability.

TRANSLATING THESE PRINCIPLES TO FAMILY LIFE

Your game worth playing can also be declared in your home. I often talk to my married crewmembers about the challenge of listening to an angry spouse while putting aside defensiveness. Listening is a great challenge when the person you deeply love is upset with you or your behavior. I point out that each of us can create a great relationship when we give up our righteousness and listen to make a difference for our loved ones. While it takes practice to release conversations of justification and blame, particularly in intimate relationships, the benefits of letting go strongly outweigh the benefits of defensiveness.

Imagine a family sitting together and declaring a vision. Let's say they choose to create a home in which people support and act lovingly toward one another. Just as in a business setting, family members can voice their personal and shared commitment to the vision. They can learn to listen to make a difference for one another as they each take responsibility for the vision. Listening skills and a willingness to hold each other accountable to the vision serve to keep a family united and growing. When people are upset with each other, they can listen from their commitment to lift up the greatness of their family members. I invite you to create and commit yourself to a powerful vision for your family. Take responsibility for sharing your vision with them, and together, make it real.

EMPOWERING SOCIAL CHANGE

I tell my friends and family how strange it is that I have written a book that encourages people to go out and make a difference at work and beyond. Honestly, for much of my life I feared people and wanted only to be left alone to run my business my way. The hurt and anger I felt throughout much of my youth led me to demand control and rob others of their power. I cannot say this enough: "If I can change, anyone can." Now I believe that you and I, as individuals, have the opportunity to make a real difference in the lives of others. I know that the principles I've shared can empower people to positively change their community and the world.

As part of my commitment to make a difference, I've volunteered to share these concepts and management principles with educational systems and schools. Since schools often don't have the financial resources to participate in our training or consultation services, I share our lessons with them, as my schedule permits, at no charge. It is my belief that to have a maximum influence in the world, young people need to define a powerful purpose, choose conversations that reinforce that purpose, and understand the difference between "being" and "doing." My efforts in the educational system have centered on helping schools empower teachers and students to that end.

One example of how these ideas are shared in schools comes from Des Moines Elementary School in Des Moines, Washington. I received a call from a friend asking me to give a presentation at a struggling elementary school. The principal of that school, Leslie Perry, advised me that they had no budget for a workshop or consultation, and I assured her that I didn't charge when it came to school systems. Ms. Perry told me that she was at a school "with declining test scores, an increasing minority status, and very high poverty." She described the situation at her school as being "in a lot of hurt." It had gotten so bad that Ms. Perry was personally buying paper supplies for her students.

Prior to my trip to Des Moines Elementary with Jim, the school's scores on state standardized testing were generally around the fiftieth percentile in reading, in the high twenties for writing, and near the thirtieth percentile in math. Leslie Perry asked her staff to take time out of their personal lives to stay until five o'clock one evening as Jim and I visited with them.

Together we discussed the teachers' vision for Des Moines Elementary School's future, and we shared stories and lessons from the World Famous Pike Place Fish Market. When the staff at Des Moines talked about their vision, they imagined an 80 percent passing rate for all elements of the state proficiency exam. I asked, "Why not one hundred percent? Which twenty percent of the children do you want to leave behind?" I shared with the teachers and staff that I have been described as both a dreamer and a fool. In either case, I knew the world famous difference we had achieved as fishmongers. I asked them to imagine what they could do if they made a commitment to be a world famous learning institution.

The caring teachers and administration at Des Moines Elementary were eager to put our ideas and suggestions into action, and what incredible success they produced! Ms. Perry appeared profoundly moved, tearful, and excited when she told me, "We were on fire thanks to your visit. The results have shown up for our kids. While our staff and student population didn't change, your message helped us with a huge breakthrough. In our first set of test scores since your visit, we saw amazing results. Our math scores went from the thirtieth percentile to the fiftieth, reading scores went from the fiftieth to the seventy-fifth percentile, and writing scores shot up from the high twenties to the sixtieth percentile. I am overjoyed by the progress we have made in such a short time with the tools and motivation you shared. Our children are all the better for your efforts."

The true reason for Des Moines Elementary School's success lies in the efforts of Leslie Perry and her team of dedicated instructors. They defined a more powerful vision and committed to it. Working together they generated success with students in every interaction each and every day. The staff served as support for one another as each teacher aspired to greatness for herself, her team members, and her students. For me, it's gratifying to see the lessons of the fish market swimming into the lives of children and the educational system. I continue to be humbled by the opportunities afforded me to make a difference.

All of us can come together and benefit from generating bold visions of the future. You have an opportunity to positively empower people. I have taken a stand for world peace as an idea whose time has come. I am committed to that vision and live that commitment daily. I invite you to create a powerful vision for yourself and others in your community.

MY PERSONAL COMMITMENT TO YOU

If Pike Place Fish can make a world famous difference from a small storefront with zero advertising in a smelly, physically challenging profession, then what's possible for you, your business, your family, and your community? How empowered, energized, and alive can you make your workplace? How willing are you to have your life truly matter?

Credits